THE
DAD BOOK

JAY PAYLEITNER

HARVEST HOUSE PUBLISHERS
EUGENE, OREGON

Cover by Left Coast Design, Portland, Oregon

Cover photo © MCarper / Shutterstock

Published in association with The Steve Laube Agency, LLC, 5025 N. Central Ave., #635, Phoenix, Arizona 85012.

THE DAD BOOK

Copyright © 2015 Jay Payleitner
Published by Harvest House Publishers
Eugene, Oregon 97402
www.harvesthousepublishers.com

ISBN 978-0-7369-6358-9 (hardcover)
ISBN 978-0-7369-6359-6 (eBook)

Printed in China

14 15 6 17 18 19 20 21 22 23 / RDS-KBD / 10 9 8 7 6 5 4 3 2 1

To my perfect grandchildren
—Judah, Jackson, and all those still to come—
and their devoted dads

Foreword
by Carey Casey

If you picked up this book because of the photo on the cover, I'm not surprised. Because that's how Jay got me to write this foreword.

Jay has been a good friend and colleague of the National Center for Fathering for more than 20 years. And he knows I've got a soft spot for dads who connect with their kids physically, emotionally, and spiritually.

When I saw the artwork for the book cover, it unleashed a flood of emotions and memories. My father had scruffy whiskers, and they were wonderful to feel. Especially when he kissed my forehead.

All kids need to feel that kind of closeness with their dads. The warmth. The security. The love. Children who enjoy a heartfelt connection with their fathers will almost always have a strong sense of confidence and personal integrity. Empowered by their father's love, they can explore the world, discover their gifts, and experience true joy.

That's right, I saw all of that in the cover photo. Did you see it too?

Then I opened the book, and it got even better. In these pages you'll find a plethora of ways you can make your own heartfelt connection with your kids. Some creative. Some old classics. Some silly. Some straightforward. A few of Jay's ideas will leave you scratching your head thinking, *How did he come up with that?* Dad, I recommend you just do it. Do it all.

I'm an old football player and sports fan, so allow me an analogy from the gridiron. Wherever you are in life, *The Dad Book* is going to give you the next play. Maybe you're a new dad and this book was a gift at a baby shower. Use this well-conceived playbook to kick off your fathering game plan. If you have school-age kids, you'll find scores of ideas to help you score big-time. Or maybe you've got surly teenagers at home and you're not even sure how to walk through their bedroom door. Don't just punt. Instead, turn to "Invisible Force Field" on page 76.

Whether you're winning as a dad or a few points behind on the scoreboard, flip through this book and find the next play to help you gain some extra yardage and many victories with your family.

So start making memories, Dad. You'll be storing up hours of game film that will bring you tears of joy and laughter for the rest of your life.

Carey Casey is CEO of the National Center for Fathering, author of *Championship Fathering*, and a dynamic speaker. He has served as chaplain for the Summer Olympics and several NFL teams. Carey and his wife, Melanie, have four children and nine grandchildren.

Introduction: The Dad Gift

If you received this book as a gift from your son or daughter, that's pretty darn fabulous. They're declaring they want you in their life. They need you. And they're counting on you to be the dad.

They truly appreciate the time you spend reading bedtime stories, catching fireflies, driving carpools, and making waffles. They honor your commitment to give noogies every day and to sit on tiny chairs sipping tea with stuffed bears and tigers.

The recipient of this book (that's you, Dad) is being elevated to hero status, which means you may be required to rescue a kid who climbs too high on the monkey bars. You may need to pick up and pay for enough pizzas to feed 23 homecoming parade float builders someday. Or you might need to race a college application to the FedEx drop box.

Dad, you may even be called on to do something you don't especially want to do, such as hunt garter snakes or get your toenails painted. Train for a 10K with your middle-schooler. Read *The Very Hungry Caterpillar* 43 nights in a row. Miss a Packers' play-off game to watch a rain-soaked youth soccer game. Or change a teen's tire on a slushy freeway.

If you received this book as a gift from your wife, that's also fabulous. She's reminding you that God has chosen you to be a dad. She's promising to help you find success in that high calling. And she's expressing confidence in your qualifications and expertise.

If you received this book as a gift from a friend, they're saying, "Congratulations." Or maybe, "Welcome to the exclusive club of fathering awesomeness."

If you bought this book as a gift for yourself, you have the luckiest kids in the world. Those kids have a dad who knows much but also knows there's much more to know!

So enjoy the magnificent and auspicious title of dad. You've earned it. Or you soon will. My prayer is this book will nudge you to explore new ideas and stretch yourself a bit. After all, Dad, you have wisdom and experience worth passing on. You have a voice that needs to be heard. And that might even mean opening this book and reading a quote, poem, fact, philosophical tidbit, or joke right out loud.

If you find something meaningful, I hope you'll pass it on as a gift to another dad, stepdad, granddad, uncle, or father figure. We're all in this together.

The alphabetical arrangement of this book will lead

you on a surprising journey, zigzagging over a lot of ground and expanding your fathering horizons. But isn't that how life as a dad rolls along? We go from serious to silly. We share a pizza then share a memory. In one 24-hour period, we might be a provider, scientist, gopher, coach, disciplinarian, storyteller, magician, theologian, comedian, and shoulder to cry on.

This is not my first book for dads. But it was the most fun to research, write, and pull together. I feel as if it was a gift to me as well.

Regardless of how you acquired this volume, there's one thing that must be acknowledged. The book is not really the gift. The gift is how a man responds to the idea of being a father. Will you accept it? Or will you set it aside? Will you see the priceless value of your fathering role? Will you unwrap such a gift, cherish it, and give it priority status in your own life?

Dad, in the end, when it comes to your children, the real gift is you.

> *The most important thing a man can know is that, as he approaches his own door, someone on the other side is listening for the sound of his footsteps.*
>
> —Clark Gable

*One of the great privileges reserved
for fathers is that when we look at
our own children, we get just a small
sampling of God's love for each of us.*

—Jay Payleitner

Aardvark

A word like "aardvark" may not seem like the most appropriate way to launch a book for dads, but stick with me.

You already know that kids like things that are cool and funny. Well, "aardvark" is both. It sounds funny. The word looks funny. And it helps that the animal also looks funny. Plus, the word is kind of cool because it features a double "A." Pretty unusual.

Worth noting. An aardwolf is a member of the hyena family, dines mostly on termites, and lives in the scrublands of eastern and southern Africa. The expression "aargh" was made popular by the occasional frustrated pirate, and Charlie Brown screamed the similar "aaugh" immediately following his annual autumn ritual of failing to kick a football.

The word "bazaar," which refers to a kind of street market, also has a double "A." If you ever find yourself in a weird street market, go ahead and say, "This is a bizarre bazaar." And then ask your grade-schooler what a homophone is and see if he or she can define and spell both versions of the word.

In the Old Testament, Abraham had a son named Isaac. The story of Abraham tying Isaac to an altar and coming quite close to stabbing him is pretty dramatic and worth reading with your kids. My wife and I named our fourth son Isaac, and it turns out that quite a few people erroneously spell his name "Issac."

Perhaps the greatest home run hitter of all time, Hank Aaron, begins his last name with a double "A." In 2007 another ballplayer allegedly used performance-enhancing drugs to break Aaron's record of 755 homers. His use of steroids may very well keep his name out of the Hall of Fame and will definitely keep it out of this book.

So did you follow all that? We started with a simple word and followed a rabbit trail to learn a new word, recall a favorite comic-strip character, ponder biblical history, inject a spelling lesson, recognize a sports hero, and open the door to a worthwhile conversation about illegal drugs and the dangers they present to your health and your legacy.

That's what dads do. We explore the world and invite our kids to join us. Often without even leaving home.

Alec, Randall, Max, Isaac, Rae Anne

The best kids in the world. You may choose to disagree.

Amble

by Chris Fabry, award-winning author and radio personality

I can't remember having many conversations with my father. We took long walks together when I was young and listened to baseball into the night when the fireflies rose. I'm sure he said things to me in those times, but I remember more about what he showed than what he said.

One of the things he showed me was how to be kind. Kindness and gentleness are in short supply today, especially from people in a hurry. But my father was rarely in a hurry. He ambled. He'd stop to look at plants and trees and point out irregularities in limbs and undergrowth. A deer peeking through from the woods or the pesky groundhog that vexed his garden.

Farm animals were comfortable with him and he with them. When he was near the end of his life, he woke up and tried to get out of the hospital bed. My sister-in-law was there to try to stop him. "You need to stay in bed," she said.

"No, I have to get up and milk the cows. Can't you hear them?"

I've always wondered which cows he heard. There was a story about him when he was a baby. He grew up in the coalfields of West Virginia in a harsh environment. His stomach couldn't handle the milk he was given, and his health began to fail. Finally, they found a cow whose milk he could tolerate. I've given thanks for that cow—not only that it sustained him but that it also allowed me a chance at life some 40 years later.

The apostle Paul encouraged his friends, "Be completely humble and gentle; be patient, bearing with one another in love" (Ephesians 4:2). My father didn't tell me those words—he lived them out with strong hands and a heart as big as his hundred-acre farm.

Anticipatory Parenting

- Move the baby wipes within reach *before* you open the diaper.

- Install outlet protectors *before* the infant starts crawling.

- Check out the schools *before* you move into a neighborhood.

- When you come home from work, get in the right frame of mind *before* you walk in the front door.

- Stash a hidden supply of poster boards and colored markers *before* your kids come to you at seven p.m., frantic about a school project due the next day.

- Encourage young teenagers to commit to sexual purity *before* their first date.

- Do the "where do babies come from" talk *before* your kids hear about it on the playground or in their school's sex-education curriculum.

- Hit the batting cages and play catch with your son or daughter a couple weeks *before* baseball or softball tryouts.

- Decide which church service you're going to as a family *before* going to bed Saturday night.

- Teach your kids dinner table etiquette— napkins in lap, what fork to use when, elbows off the table—*before* going to the fancy restaurant or reception.

- Teach your son how to tie a tie *before* prom night.

- Train up your children in the way they should go *before* turning them loose on the world, and when they are old they will not depart from it (Proverbs 22:6, paraphrased).

- Demonstrate defensive driving, review the financial aspects of car insurance, and establish that driving is not a right, but a privilege…*before* they get their license.

- Give a quick call to the hosting parents *before* dropping off your kid at a sleepover.

- Put your kids' birthdays, concerts, and game schedules on your calendar *before* making any other appointments.

- Lead your children to trust God and explain how Jesus will "prepare a place" for them… *before* they face eternity (see John 14:1-3).

Apple Picking, Etc.

Once a year in your part of the world there is a popular annual event that has a good chance of being an amusing annual family excursion. The best part is you don't have to remember it. The media will remind you. Because this event is in your area, it's probably a simple day trip you can afford to do every year. Which makes it a tradition. And kids love traditions.

Here in the Midwest, it's visiting an apple orchard. On the Oregon Coast, it might be clam digging in the fall when tides are low. Officially, May is National Strawberry Month, but New Englanders pick strawberries in June. If you live near our nation's capital, early April ushers in the National Cherry Blossom Festival. The Indy 500 is Memorial Day weekend. The Masters Golf Tournament, at Augusta National in Georgia, is always booked for the weekend ending with the third Sunday in June.

Might you be a bird-watching family? The swallows return to San Juan Capistrano, California, each year around March 19, and the buzzards return to Hinckley Ridge, Ohio, every March 15.

The Iditarod sets out from Anchorage in early March. The UFO Festival is in Roswell, New Mexico, in early July. Scattered across the country are hot-air balloon races, storytelling festivals, and Renaissance faires that might be worth checking out.

Down south, New Orleans has Mardi Gras, and Daytona Beach has Spring Break. But on second thought, those events are not exactly family friendly.

With a little research you can probably find annual events within a few hours' drive that will expose your kids to art, music, books, film, or dance. Or maybe your annual family tradition is to spend a day at your own county or state fair. That's actually a pretty sweet choice. Cotton candy and elephant ears for everyone!

> *My father used to play with my brother and me in the yard. Mother would come out and say, You're tearing up the grass. We're not raising grass, Dad would reply. We're raising boys.*
>
> —Harmon Killebrew

Babysitting

Once and for all, fathers do not babysit their kids. Fathers can watch their kids. Spend time with them. And even be stuck with them. But they're *your* kids. Grandmas, aunts, big brothers, big sisters, and the teenager from down the street can babysit your kids. But dads should never say, "I'm babysitting." Rant over.

Banana Sliced in the Peel

Have you heard about the new bananas being grown specifically for people who plan to put them in cereal? Well, neither has your kid. Next April Fool's Day or anytime, introduce your child to the appealing concept of organic, sliced bananas with a little pre-slicing monkey business.

Get a banana and a long needle or a hat pin. Stick the pin into the peel someplace near the top. Wiggle it left and right, slicing the fruit without disturbing the far side of the peel. Pull the pin out, move it a little lower, and repeat the process several times.

When the family sits down for breakfast, launch into a tale of the astonishing benefits of genetic food engineering and then pass the banana to your kid to peel for himself. He'll be stupefied as the perfectly sliced pieces drop into his bowl.[1]

Bat House

My son Isaac bought me a bat house one year for Father's Day. What a great gift. It would have been so cool to watch bats fly in and out and to know they were eating tons of mosquitoes. I researched online where and how to hang it. But I never did. That bat house is still in my garage. That's something I regret. I'm sorry, Isaac.

Being Brave at Night

The other night 'bout two o'clock, or
    maybe it was three,
An elephant with shining tusks came
    chasing after me.
His trunk was wavin' in the air an' spoutin'
    jets of steam
An' he was out to eat me up, but still I didn't
    scream
Or let him see that I was scared—a better
    thought I had,
I just escaped from where I was and crawled
    in bed with Dad.

One time there was a giant who was horri-
    ble to see,
He had three heads and twenty arms, an' he
    came after me
And red hot fire came from his mouths and
    every hand was red
And he declared he'd grind my bones and
    make them into bread.
But I was just too smart for him, I fooled
    him mighty bad,
Before his hands could collar me I crawled
    in bed with Dad.

I ain't scared of nothin' that comes pesterin'
    me at night.
Once I was chased by forty ghosts all shim-
    mery an' white.
An' I just raced 'em round the room an' let
    'em think maybe
I'd have to stop an' rest awhile, when they
    could capture me.
Then when they leapt onto my bed, Oh Gee!
    But they were mad
To find that I had slipped away an' crawled
    in bed with Dad.

No giants, ghosts or elephants have dared to
    come in there
'Cuz if they did he'd beat 'em up and chase
    'em to their lair.
They just hang 'round the children's rooms
    an' snap an' snarl an' bite
An' laugh if they can make 'em yell for help
    with all their might.
But I don't ever yell out loud. I'm not that
    sort of lad,
I slip from out the covers and I crawl in bed
    with Dad.

—Edgar Guest[2]

Bioluminescence*

A chemical reaction inside the thorax of the lightning bug causes bioluminescence. Specifically, oxygen combines with calcium, adenosine triphosphate (ATP), and the chemical luciferin in the presence of luciferase, a bioluminescent enzyme. Unlike a lightbulb, which produces heat, a firefly's light is "cold light." Which is nice because otherwise, the firefly would burn itself up.

There are several theories of why fireflies light up. Their bodies produce defensive steroids, making them unpalatable to predators, and their flashing may serve as a warning display, communicating their distastefulness. Also, the flash patterns of adult fireflies likely serve as a way to attract members of the opposite sex.

Or maybe fireflies are God's gift to dads and kids to make memories on warm summer evenings.

(Worth noting: One of my editors, Paul, stunned me with the information that for the most part, fireflies

---

* Things dads should know just in case the kids ask.

west of the Rockies don't flash. Which proves that dads don't know everything. And that's okay.)

Birthdates

When I was growing up, my dad could not recite the birthdays of his four kids. That was stunning to me. I knew my siblings' birthdays at a very young age: Mary Kay's birthday was February 3, Mark's was March 24, Susie's was July 16, and mine was June 6. I was so stunned at my dad's ignorance that I briefly questioned his commitment as a father.

I have since forgiven him. Mostly because if you asked me the birthdates of my five kids, I would have to think very hard. I believe I could do it. But I have gotten them wrong in the past. And I always have to ask Rita the year of their births. She knows instantly.

Boneheaded Remarks

"Because I said so."

"If your brother jumped off a bridge, would you?"

"If you break your leg, don't come running to me."

"Look at me when I'm talking to you."

"Don't look at me like that."

"Don't cross your eyes—they'll stay that way."

"Stop crying or I'll give you something to cry about."

"Money doesn't grow on trees."

"Were you born in a barn?"

"It's all fun and games until someone gets hurt."

"Do you think your socks are going to pick themselves up?"

"What are you waiting for, an engraved invitation?"

"Two wrongs do not make a right."

"You're the oldest. You should know better."

"What did I just get finished telling you?"

"Don't ever let me catch you doing that again."

"I didn't ask who put it there, I said, 'Pick it up!'"

"Pick that up before somebody trips on it and breaks their neck!"

"If I want your opinion, I'll ask for it!"

"If you're bored, I can always find something for you to do."

"Life isn't supposed to be fair."

"I paid good money for that."

"Don't make me stop this car!"

Breakfast in Bed

Heard in passing:

On Father's Day, a little boy surprises his dad with

breakfast in bed—cold and runny scrambled eggs, blackened toast, and coffee with grounds floating across the surface. The dad doesn't want to hurt his son's feelings, so he takes a breath and wolfs down the eggs and toast and begins to wash it down with the gritty coffee. Suddenly the dad realizes there are two plastic army men in the bottom of the cup.

"What's this?" he says.

The boy smiles proudly and sings, "The best part of waking up is soldiers in your cup!"

Budweiser Bedsheets

Somehow at some fund-raising event, my parents won a door prize that probably never should have come through our front door. It was a twin set of single-bed sheets and matching pillowcases featuring giant Budweiser logos. They were exactly the right size for the bunk beds where my brother and I slept. Go figure. So most of my fourth and fifth grade year, the Budweiser logo was the last image I saw before drifting off to sleep.

When I was growing up, my parents shared an adult beverage with friends once or twice a month. I never remember them getting drunk. So maybe they really didn't see the absurdity in tucking their sons into Budweiser dreamland. Still, it seems like something most dads would want to avoid. Would you agree?

*The supreme happiness of life
is the conviction that we are loved.*

—*Victor Hugo*

Cc

Career Counseling

Are you the kind of dad who steers your kids toward practical careers, such as business, engineering, nursing, or accounting?

Well, what if your son or daughter is an artist at heart? Or has a legitimate chance to make it as an athlete, musician, or actor? What if their heart tells them to pursue a soul-satisfying career that is completely outside your own area of expertise? Forest ranger. Bricklayer. Archaeologist. Audio engineer.

One of the most frequently quoted passages of Scripture regarding how you might help guide your child's career is Proverbs 22:6—"Train up a child in the way he should go, even when he is old he will not depart from it" (NASB).

That's a solid parenting strategy. But perhaps even more important is this idea from the book of Titus. Whatever career path they choose, we need to challenge them to "be an example of good deeds, with purity in doctrine, dignified, sound in speech which is beyond reproach…to be well-pleasing, not argumentative, not pilfering…to deny ungodliness and worldly desires and to live sensibly, righteously and godly in the present age" (Titus 2:7-12 NASB).

Whether our sons and daughters become artists or astronauts, surgeons or sailors, teachers or truck drivers, are not these attributes exactly what we want for them?

Carousels

This book contains a flurry of quotations to ponder. One of my favorites deserves some additional consideration.

> You don't really understand human nature unless you know why a child on a merry-go-round will wave at his parents every time around—and why his parents will always wave back.
>
> —William D. Tammeus

That quote is a snapshot of kids growing up and parents letting go.

A child does something daring. In this case, it's straddling a painted pony and enduring a cacophony of garish colors and noise. They're no longer holding onto Dad's strong hand or Mom's secure apron strings. Suddenly, they are whooshed out of sight. They're gone. On their own.

But what happens on each revolution? As they come full circle, they look for you and loosen their grip with one hand just long enough to wave with delight.

The only reason a small child has such courage is that they know you will be there in case they need to be rescued. Seeing you standing firm at every revolution provides the security *they* need and confirms the heart connection *you* need. The exuberant wave is not hello or goodbye—it's saying, "We're in this together."

So. Remember the carousel.

Embrace that image when your children do anything daring. Kindergarten. Their first sleepover. Summer camp. Their first date. Their first job. College. The mission field. The military. Be there to send them off and welcome them back. And stand firm every minute in between.

Casey at the Bat

The outlook wasn't brilliant for the Mudville
nine that day:

The score stood four to two, with but one
    inning more to play,
And then when Cooney died at first, and
    Barrows did the same,
A pall-like silence fell upon the patrons of
    the game.

A straggling few got up to go in deep despair.
    The rest
Clung to the hope which springs eternal in
    the human breast;
They thought, "If only Casey could but get a
    whack at that—
We'd put up even money now, with Casey at
    the bat."

But Flynn preceded Casey, as did also
    Jimmy Blake,
And the former was a lulu, while the latter
    was a cake;
So upon that stricken multitude grim mel-
    ancholy sat,
For there seemed but little chance of Casey
    getting to the bat.

But Flynn let drive a single, to the wonder-
    ment of all,

And Blake, the much despised, tore the
    cover off the ball;
And when the dust had lifted, and men saw
    what had occurred,
There was Jimmy safe at second and Flynn
    a-hugging third.

Then from five thousand throats and more
    there rose a lusty yell;
It rumbled through the valley, it rattled in
    the dell;
It pounded on the mountain and recoiled
    upon the flat,
For Casey, mighty Casey, was advancing to
    the bat.

There was ease in Casey's manner as he
    stepped into his place;
There was pride in Casey's bearing and a
    smile lit Casey's face.
And when, responding to the cheers, he
    lightly doffed his hat,
No stranger in the crowd could doubt 'twas
    Casey at the bat.

Ten thousand eyes were on him as he
    rubbed his hands with dirt;

Five thousand tongues applauded when he
    wiped them on his shirt;
Then while the writhing pitcher ground the
    ball into his hip,
Defiance flashed in Casey's eye, a sneer
    curled Casey's lip.

And now the leather-covered sphere came
    hurtling through the air,
And Casey stood a-watching it in haughty
    grandeur there.
Close by the sturdy batsman the ball
    unheeded sped—
"That ain't my style," said Casey. "Strike one!"
    the umpire said.

From the benches, black with people, there
    went up a muffled roar,
Like the beating of the storm-waves on a
    stern and distant shore;
"Kill him! Kill the umpire!" shouted some-
    one on the stand;
And it's likely they'd have killed him had not
    Casey raised his hand.

With a smile of Christian charity great
    Casey's visage shone;

He stilled the rising tumult; he bade the
game go on;
He signaled to the pitcher, and once more
the dun sphere flew;
But Casey still ignored it and the umpire
said, "Strike two!"

"Fraud!" cried the maddened thousands, and
echo answered "Fraud!"
But one scornful look from Casey and the
audience was awed.
They saw his face grow stern and cold, they
saw his muscles strain,
And they knew that Casey wouldn't let that
ball go by again.

The sneer is gone from Casey's lip, his teeth
are clenched in hate,
He pounds with cruel violence his bat upon
the plate;
And now the pitcher holds the ball, and now
he lets it go,
And now the air is shattered by the force of
Casey's blow.

Oh, somewhere in this favoured land the
sun is shining bright,

The band is playing somewhere, and some-
　　where hearts are light;
And somewhere men are laughing, and
　　somewhere children shout,
But there is no joy in Mudville—mighty
　　Casey has struck out.

　　　　　　　　　—Ernest Lawrence Thayer

Caterpillar

This short list is in honor of my daughter-in-law, Kaitlin, who works for Caterpillar, the makers of the world's most awesome land-moving equipment. Remember, Dad…

Backhoes scoop.
Front loaders lift.

Dozers push.
Tractors move.
Rollers flatten.
Compactors settle.
Graders scrape, level, and slope.

Kaitlin totally understands when laymen get some of the names and functions wrong. So, Dad, you're forgiven for not knowing the exact words to describe all those big yellow vehicles. But you're not forgiven if you have a toddler and don't pull over once in a while when you come upon a construction site to watch the big rigs roll. The most fun is actually to watch your toddler watch.

Checkerboard Squares

Ask your kid how many squares are on a checkerboard. It's a great chance to teach them the rhyme "Eight times eight fell on the floor. I picked it up, it was sixty-four." But of course, if they say sixty-four, you'll want to point out there 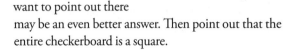 may be an even better answer. Then point out that the entire checkerboard is a square.

They may roll their eyes. Or they may say, "Okay, sixty-five."

Then, of course, you ask, "Are there any other squares? Maybe squares that are two by two? Squares that are three by three? Four by four? Five by five? Six by six? Seven by seven?" The actual total is a whopping 204. And, yes, many of the squares are a little tricky to count because there are eight different sizes, and they all overlap. Here's the math:

> 64 squares are 1 by 1.
> 49 squares are 2 by 2.
> 36 squares are 3 by 3.
> 25 squares are 4 by 4.
> 16 squares are 5 by 5.
> 9 squares are 6 by 6.
> 4 squares are 7 by 7.
> 1 square is 8 by 8.

With any brainteasers, Dad, the goal is never to make your kids feel stupid. The goal is to empower them to see how they can approach a challenging question from different angles. The answer "sixty-four" is not wrong. Creativity trainers promote the idea of "looking for the next right answer." Express that concept to your child, and if their eyes light up with curiosity, give them examples.

Thomas Edison failed 10,000 times before finding the right filament for the lightbulb that would burn for 1200 hours rather than fizzling out in seconds.

Henry Ford had a vision for a more efficient way of building motorcars. Instead of a factory floor where small groups of workers built one car at time, he invented the moving assembly line. The Ford factory was soon producing one car every 93 minutes. He made cars affordable to the general public and doubled the minimum wage for his workers.

Samuel Colt—at age 16—saw how the steering wheel of a ship revolved and locked into place. He envisioned a handgun that could hold multiple rounds of ammunition with revolving chambers. It took a few years, but the Colt Revolver began production in 1836.

French philosopher Émile Chartier summed up the perils of settling for the first right answer when he said, "Nothing is more dangerous than an idea when it's the only one you have."

So next time your kids face a creative conundrum, encourage them to look for the next right answer. That could be a short story idea for language arts, a theme for a party, a gift for Mom, a hairstyle, a face-painting inspiration, a snowman design, a plan for a scarecrow, or an idea for a science fair project. You'll want to give an initial dose of acknowledgment and praise to the first solid idea they come up with. But then challenge them to invest additional time to see if there's a better way. A totally new way—a way that only they could think of!

Color-Wheel Wisdom

Every kid has a box of ten or more Crayola markers in their backpack, so many art teachers don't bother teaching students the astonishing process of mixing paint to make new colors.

In theory, when working in watercolors or tempera paint, you only need black, white, and the three primary colors (red, blue, and yellow). All the other colors can be created from those basic hues.

red + yellow = orange
red + blue = purple
blue + yellow = green

black + white = gray
red + white = pink
yellow + red + blue = brown

The intensity, opacity, and vibrancy are all determined by varying proportions. Begin with a small amount of the lighter color and add small amounts of the darker pigment, mixing as you go.

Why is this important? First, it's just cool. You don't have orange paint, and then suddenly you do have orange paint! Even better, your young artist can paint that green crocodile or pink elephant without Dad making a late-evening trip across town to the hobby store that's probably closed anyway.

Confidence

by Matt Guevara, executive director of International Network of Children's Ministry

I'll never forget my dad and mom dropping me off for college. We walked around campus, and they got me settled in. But when it came time to say goodbye, I was struck by the significance of how my life was about to change. They had been wonderful parents, and suddenly I would be on my own. In the moment, I was unprepared and began to cry. My dad looked me in the eye and said, "You can do this. If you need help, I'll be here." That was a pivotal moment for me.

Contradicting Mom

Never in front of the kids. Rarely when the kids are infants or toddlers. And even as your kids get older, make it a priority to be on the same page with their mom when discussing limits, discipline, priorities, curfews, and expectations. This principle is especially true if Mom and Dad have different addresses.

> *Parents are heroes already—all they have to do is start acting like it.*
>
> *—Josh McDowell*

Daughters Dating

Heard in passing:

A good friend of mine warned me that as my three daughters became old enough to date, I'd disapprove of every young man who took them out. When the time came, I was pleased that my friend's prediction was wrong. Each boy was pleasant and well mannered. Talking to my daughter Joanna one day, I said that I liked all the young men she and her sisters brought home.

"You know, Dad," she replied, "we don't show you everybody."

Dinnertime

You've heard the goal of eating dinner as a family. But let me take it a step further. As your kids get older, their schedules become even more unpredictable than yours. In a perfect world, you might like to sit down at exactly six every evening. But if your family sometimes eats at four thirty and sometimes eats at nine fifteen, it's really okay. Never lay a shred of guilt on any individual for compelling you to eat at weird hours.

Regardless of when you sit down, take a moment,

grasp hands, look at each face around the table, and give thanks to the Provider for the food and the family.

Driver's Ed

Instructors in high schools and storefront driving schools will do a pretty good job teaching your young teenager how to use turn signals and change lanes properly. But, Dad, when you're in the passenger seat and they're behind the wheel with a learner's permit in their wallet, you can't emphasize these three driving essentials enough.

1. *No tailgating.* "Let's ease back from that guy's bumper."

2. *Check blind spots.* "Somehow cars disappear when they're right behind you in the next lane. You can't just use your mirrors. You have to actually turn your head."

3. *Wear seat belts.* "Not wearing your seat belt is like telling your family you don't care about us. We're the ones who will be visiting you in the hospital or going to your funeral."

And if the driver-in-training whines or screams back at you, calmly tell them to stop the car, switch places, and you drive home.

Duty of the Moment

The baby spikes a fever and can't go to the sitter.

With no self-pity or fanfare, you step up, cancel a couple appointments, and take care of your little one.

Twenty minutes before the game begins, your son realizes he forgot the belt to his baseball pants.

You race home and race back to the diamond—only to discover he borrowed a belt from a teammate. It's okay, Dad.

Your young teenage daughter unexpectedly needs a feminine hygiene product. Without asking questions, you make the dash to Walgreen's and never mention it again.

Your high-school senior realizes the college application was supposed to be *received* at the school by October 15. Not *postmarked* by October 15. While she scrambles to assemble the paperwork, you locate the nearest FedEx drop box with the extra-late pickup.

On a first date, your son texts from the restaurant that he's short of cash. Secretly, you meet him at the maître d's desk with a couple twenties. (He'll pay you back later.)

You're expecting a quiet Friday evening at home with the missus. Your son texts that the football game is rained out and he's bringing some soggy friends home. Somehow you also spring for four extra-large pizzas.

Your daughter and son-in-law tweet that their new home apparently is on a flood plain. Twenty minutes later, you show up at their door with a portable water pump, two dehumidifiers, and a mop.

It's good to be the hero. It's even better to be the quiet, unassuming hero.

Echelons*

Ornithologists point to two probable explanations for the V-shaped flight formations of geese. One is that the birds are conserving energy by taking advantage of the upwash vortex

---

* Things dads should know just in case the kids ask.

currents created by the wings of the birds in front. The other is that the formation facilitates orientation and communication. Photographs of echelons have measured bird positions and found them to be almost always located in a way that would give them some energetic advantage. In addition, knowledge of birds' visual axes, blind spots, and field of vision indicate that the birds' formation may allow for optimal visual alignment in flight.

Echoes

"You make me smile."

"I am so proud of you."

"Where did you learn to do that? That's fantastic."

"I look around and can't believe how lucky I am to be part of this family."

"You are a gift from God."

"You're amazing."

"You did that! That's epic."

"Well played."

"Nice."

"You probably don't even realize how much your little brother looks up to you."

"You are just about the best thing that ever happened to me!"

"That's a great idea."

"I was thinking about you all day today."
"You know what? I love you."

"What's wrong with you?"
"Can't you do anything right?"
"Why can't you be more like your sister?"
"That's pretty much what I expected from you."
"Won't you ever learn?"
"That's the dumbest thing I ever saw."
"I didn't raise you that way."
"Then don't bother coming home."

Entitlements

by Tim Hollinger, audio engineer
and technology manager

My dad recognized the rewards and personal satisfaction that come from hard work, earning your daily bread, and providing for your family. He used to say, "Firewood warms you more than once—when you cut it, split it, stack it, carry it, and burn it."

Entomology

Mom wants you to squash the invader. But before killing the centipede on the kitchen counter, trap it under a clear glass and ask your son or daughter to

identify it. You can certainly look it up on the Internet, but first see if you can recall some entomology from your middle-school biology class. Explain that an insect has three body parts—head, thorax, abdomen—and six legs. Spiders have two body parts with eight legs. Worms have multiple segments with no legs. A centipede has a segmented body with up to thirty-four legs. Observe it for a while. Finally, make Mom happy by squishing it and making sure no guts residue remains.

Etymology

Mom wants you to squash another invader. But before killing the centipede on the kitchen counter, trap it under a clear glass and find out if your son or daughter can determine the origin of its name. Explain how words can often be broken down in parts. *Centi* + *pede*. Remind your pint-size linguist there are 100 *cents* in a dollar and 100 years in a *century*. Also, you *pedal* a bike with your feet, and people who walk down the street are called *pedestrians*. So "centipede" means "100 feet." Observe your newly named centipede for a while. Finally, make Mom happy by squishing it, once again making sure no guts residue remains.

Expectations

Kids don't need parents to nag or whine. They don't need daily ultimatums or constant reminders. And they certainly don't need parents to lay guilt trips on them. But they do want to know what is expected of them.

Set reasonable expectations early and often—by

example or mandate—and watch them respond with enthusiasm. Some of the following is common courtesy. Some is basic hygiene. Some is simple economics. All of it is groundwork for life. Feel free to add your own. Expect your kids to…

refrain from smoking

turn the lights out when they leave a room

hang up their clothes

put their cereal bowls in the dishwasher

put their soda cans in the recycling

replace the empty toilet paper roll

wipe their feet when they come inside

ask before inviting friends over

write thank-you notes

write down phone messages

pitch in around the house before large family gatherings

wear seat belts

brush their teeth twice a day

call you when they arrive at a distant destination

tell you where they're going whenever they leave the house

get up for church on Sunday morning

graduate high school

graduate college

provide you with perfect grandkids someday

> *Fathers, do not exasperate your children;*
> *instead, bring them up in the*
> *training and instruction of the Lord.*
>
> —*Ephesians 6:4*

Ff

Falling Down

by Don Smith,
Springfield, Illinois

I'm a father of five. My advice to other dads is to remember that no one learns to walk without falling down—a lot. Make sure you are the one to help your children get back on their feet so they can take another step. Don't discourage. Instead, encourage. Don't dwell on negatives; give positive feedback. You cannot expect them to be the best at something overnight. But you can expect them to be a little better than they were yesterday.

Father-of-the-Bride Songs

"Unforgettable," Natalie Cole and Nat King Cole
"Isn't She Lovely?" Stevie Wonder
"Somewhere over the Rainbow," Israel "IZ" Kamakawiwo'ole
"In My Life," The Beatles
"Cinderella," Steven Curtis Chapman
"What a Wonderful World," Louis Armstrong
"My Father's Eyes," Eric Clapton
"Lullabye" (Goodnight My Angel), Billy Joel
"I Loved Her First," Heartland
"Through the Years," Kenny Rogers
"Butterfly Kisses," Bob Carlisle

Father's Day Facts

In 1909, Mrs. Sonora Smart Dodd got the idea of celebrating Father's Day while listening to a Mother's Day sermon at her church. Her father, William Jackson Smart of Spokane, Washington, was a widower who raised six children after his wife died giving birth to the youngest.

On July 19, 1910, the governor of Washington State proclaimed the first statewide Father's Day.

In 1916, President Woodrow Wilson approved the idea of observing an annual Father's Day.

In 1924, President Calvin Coolidge made Father's Day a national event.

In 1966, President Lyndon Johnson signed a presidential proclamation declaring the third Sunday of June as Father's Day.

In 1972, President Richard Nixon signed a proclamation finally making Father's Day a federal holiday.

Hallmark has been producing Father's Day cards since the early 1920s.

The US Open always concludes on Father's Day.

Father's Day is the fifth-largest card-sending holiday in the world.

According to MarketWatch, Americans spend more than $13 billion on Father's Day gifts.

The most popular gift is not a gadget, tool, or tie. The number one gift on Father's Day is a special outing, such as a sporting event or dinner.

Forgiveness

No one could really say why he ran away. Or perhaps he didn't, but was kicked out of his home by his father for something foolish that he said or did. Either way, Paco found himself wandering the streets of Madrid, Spain, with hopes of entering into a profession that would most likely get him killed—bullfighting. Those who train under a mentor have a good chance of surviving this profession, but Paco's memory of his mistakes and guilt over what happened blindly drove him to this one-way street to suicide.

But that was the last thing his father wanted, which is why he tried something desperate which he desperately hoped would work. There was little to no chance that he would be able to find Paco by wandering the streets of Madrid, so instead he put an advertisement in the local newspaper, *El Liberal*. The advertisement read, "Paco, meet me at the Hotel Montana at noon on Tuesday. All is forgiven! Love, Papa."

Paco is such a common name in Spain that when the father went to the Hotel Montana the next day at noon there were 800 young men named Paco waiting for their fathers…and waiting for the forgiveness they never thought was possible!

—Lane Palmer [3]

Freedom

When I was a kid my parents made me choose one sport. They wanted no part of the nonsense where parents need a PhD in logistics to fit it all in, with a music lesson in the car on the way to each of the day's five after-school sports. One sport. I was nine and I was torn. In front of me was baseball, tennis, soccer and gymnastics. I remember cleaning the garage with my dad—the chore I hated then but love now because I can actually view progress—and we were talking about the decision. He loved gymnastics and was actually my coach. Though I didn't want to disappoint him, I didn't really love the sport. Sensing this tension, he stopped me mid sweep and said, "I want you to know that whatever you do, whatever you choose, I support you 100 percent and will do my best to help you do whatever that is." He probably doesn't remember that moment, but that little "talk" saved a lifetime of living up to the expectations of someone else. It gave me great freedom and confidence to be who I am today.

—Bradley Hasemeyer [4]

The Frogs and the Well

The beloved ancient Greek storyteller Aesop gave us this classic fable with a valuable moral for all ages.

Two frogs lived together in a marsh. One hot summer the marsh dried up, so they went in search of another place to live. By and by they came to a deep well. Looking down into it, one frog said to the other, "This looks like a nice cool place. Let's jump in and settle here."

But the other, who had a wiser head on his frog shoulders, replied, "Not so fast, my friend. Suppose this well dried up like the marsh. How should we get out again?"

Moral: Look before you leap.

When I was a boy of fourteen, my father was so ignorant I could hardly stand to have the old man around. But when I got to be twenty-one, I was astonished at how much the old man had learned in seven years.

—Mark Twain

Generosity

by John Bomberger, publishing executive

My dad said many times, "When they pass the plate, put something in it." As I got older, I came to understand that meant much more than simply being generous when they pass the offering basket in church. If you allow yourself to see them, God will reveal many opportunities to give back. My dad lived that truth. He was constantly aware of the needs of others and graciously generous with his time, talents, and financial resources.

A Good Son

Heard in passing:

An old gentleman living alone wants to plant his annual tomato garden, but the ground is hard and his only son, Vincent, who had worked side by side with him in the garden for many years, is in prison. The old man writes a letter to his son, describing his predicament.

Dear Vincent,

I am a little sad this spring because it looks like I won't be able to plant my tomato garden. I'm just getting too old to be digging up a garden plot. I wish you were here to turn over the hard soil for me, like in the old days.

Love, Papa

A few days later he receives a letter from his son.

Dear Papa,

Don't dig up that garden. That's where the bodies are buried.

Love, Vinnie

At four o'clock the next morning, FBI agents arrive and dig up the entire area without finding any bodies.

As they leave, they apologize to the old man for the mess. A couple days later, the old man receives another letter from his son.

> Dear Papa,
>
> Go ahead and plant the tomatoes now. That's the best I could do under the circumstances.
>
> Your loving son, Vinnie

Grammar Lessons

- Eliminate commas, that are, not necessary.
- It is wrong to ever split an infinitive.
- No sentence fragments.
- Never use a preposition to end a sentence with.
- Proofread carefully to see if you any words out.
- "I before E"—except after "C" or when you happen to be planning a feisty heist on a weird beige foreign neighbor.

Greasy Spoons

Whenever you're on a family trip or a one-on-one outing with one of your kids, make it a point to seek

out mom-and-pop diners. For better or worse, chalk it up to making memories.

Your kids will not remember the two hundredth McDonald's drive-through or the Cracker Barrel restaurant in Savannah that's nearly identical to the other 600-plus Cracker Barrels in the world. Going to Denny's, Applebee's, or IHOP is safe. But safe and predictable are not the reasons children need to take family road trips or hang with Dad.

Your kids will remember the place where the jukebox played only Dolly Parton or the special of the day was pickled pig's snout. Forever they will quote the waitress who stuck her pencil up in her babushka, called your son "sweetie pie," and yelled your entire order in greasy-spoon slang to Festus, the short-order cook.

Dad, when it comes to greasy spoons, I hope you have your own list of memories to make you smile. I encourage you to share them with your kids. As for me, I can still picture the Coffee Cup restaurant in Clinton-ville, Wisconsin. When I was a kid, it was the halfway stop for the annual Payleitner caravan heading north to the cottages on Pine Lake. Then there's the Greek diner in Rockford, Illinois. That's where, during a break in one of Isaac's club soccer tournaments, I first told him where babies come from. And I'll never forget the just-off-the-tollway diner in Pennsylvania where Alec for-got his Dodgers baseball cap. We drove back 30 miles to retrieve it.

Oh, and most of the time, the spoons are not liter-ally greasy. But sometimes, wonderfully, they are.

> *Parents are often so busy with the physical*
> *rearing of children that they miss the*
> *glory of parenthood, just as the grandeur*
> *of the trees is lost when raking leaves.*
>
> —*Marcelene Cox*

Haiku

Noogies, lightning bugs,
Frogs, mud pies, and ghost stories.
That's why kids need dads.

Is your wallet full
Of old faded school photos?
You must be a dad.

A secret for dads:
Playing rock, paper, scissors,
Kids throw scissors first.

You spend 18 years
Getting them ready to leave.
Then you're not ready.

Remember: Do not
Exasperate your children,
Or they will lose heart.

Hey, Coach

Even if your son or daughter is a terrible athlete. Even if you're a nonathlete. And especially if you're way too busy to even consider it. Step up and volunteer to coach one of your child's teams for at least one season.

Buy yourself a whistle and clipboard. Let the league commissioner assign you a roster filled with ragtag kids of all shapes, sizes, and abilities (just like a Disney movie). And then give it all you got.

Of course, if you have no clue about the rules for lacrosse or rugby (or have never even watched a game), please don't volunteer to be the head coach of a team of 14-year-olds. You don't want a posse of angry parents screaming obscenities at you for an entire season. But any dad can coach a team of second-graders in soccer or T-ball. And if you're not up for the role of head coach, then volunteer to assist. Or schedule practices. Or keep statistics. Or rake the field. (Just don't volunteer to do snacks. Real men don't organize snacks. That's what team moms are for.)

The benefits are many. You get to see your child in a new environment. You get to be close to the action, watching them grimace, grit their teeth, sweat, breathe, and stare down their opponent. As their coach, you are forced to spend time with them. In the car. On the bench. Waiting out late refs and rain delays. Your young star (or non-star) gets to see you at your best and your worst.

If your son or daughter continues on to a trophy-winning career complete with scholarships and pro contracts, you can take all the credit. You were there at the start. On the other hand, if they are just terrible and you are an even worse coach, cut your losses after one season. But have no regrets. You'll have something to laugh about together—especially when they find excellence and redemption in some other nonsporting arena.

No matter what, hang that whistle on your tie rack and let it remind you of that memorable season you spent as your kid's coach.[5]

Hold Your Baby

It's impossible to spoil a baby who is less than six months old. When they cry, pick them up. They're either wet, hungry, scared, too hot, too cold, or not feeling well. Crying babies are not attempting to manipulate you. They have a need, and you have the God-given privilege of meeting that need. It might be something serious, but it's much more likely they just want to be held. And that's not a bad thing.

Please note: You're reading this in a book for dads. Yes, it's true that Mommy reads baby signals better than you. She is also softer and cuddlier. But babies especially like the strong, firm security of being in Daddy's arms, so…Hold. Your. Baby.

Hollywood

If you thought Hollywood was in the entertainment business, you would be wrong. Hollywood is in the moneymaking business. And the way to make money is to make movies that connect with the audience. Movies that resonate with as many people as possible. Studios invest a lot of money researching the best way to emotionally connect with their audience. Even if movie scripts go off the deep end and fill the heads of filmgoers with dangerous or ludicrous notions, movie producers are usually on the right track when it comes to knowing what topics trigger the greatest emotional response of ticket buyers. And that topic is fatherhood.

Following are just a few of the movies in which the

motivation of the main character is driven by a broken or challenging relationship with his or her father. Or the main character is a man discovering new purpose in his role as a father.

Star Wars, Spiderman, Superman, Mary Poppins, Mrs. Doubtfire, Forrest Gump, Life Is Beautiful, Seabiscuit, Matchstick Men, Rain Man, Hook, Jerry McGuire, The Natural, Tommy Boy, The Descendants, The Sound of Music, Prisoners, The Judge, Now You See Me, War of the Worlds, Noah, Big Daddy, Top Gun, Home Alone, Breaking Away, Friday Night Lights, The Lion King, Stand by Me, Legends of the Fall, Jurassic Park, Paper Moon, Traffic, City Slickers, Barry Lyndon, The Champ, Ordinary People, About Schmidt, Armageddon, Austin Powers, A River Runs Through It, Over the Top, Footloose, Houseboat, Sleepless in Seattle, Field of Dreams, The Princess Diaries, The Little Mermaid, October Sky, Ferris Bueller's Day Off, The Santa Clause, It's a Wonderful Life, Raising Arizona, National Lampoon's Vacation, Mr. Mom, Three Men and a Baby, Parenthood, A Goofy Movie, Jack Frost, The Great Santini, Analyze This, Back to the Future, Dead Poets Society, Father of the Bride, Meet the Parents, The Road to Perdition, Minority Report, Signs, Taken, Sixteen Candles, Indiana Jones and the Last Crusade, Zoolander, Draft Day, Aladdin, The Rookie, Kramer vs. Kramer, About a Boy, The Shining, Catch Me If You Can, Rebel Without a Cause, We Were Soldiers, Hulk, Finding

Nemo, After Earth, Silver Linings Playbook, The Incredibles, Courageous, Trouble with the Curve, Ransom, Jaws, Paper Moon, Dirty Dancing, Prisoners, Million Dollar Baby, Cheaper by the Dozen, Nebraska, Boyhood, How to Train Your Dragon, Mystic River, Frequency, Along Came Polly, Shark Tale, Godzilla, Simon Birch, Night at the Museum, The Italian Job, Chasing Liberty, Big Fish, Elf, The Pursuit of Happyness...

And the list goes on. Some of these—*Mrs. Doubtfire, Father of the Bride, Kramer vs. Kramer, Sleepless in Seattle*—feature a big-name actor portraying a dad at a critical turning point (Robin Williams, Steve Martin, Dustin Hoffman, Tom Hanks).

Many movies, while not initially obvious, are unexpectedly about sons or daughters coming to terms with their strained relationships with their fathers. In *Top Gun*, Tom Cruise plays Maverick, the hotshot pilot who finally understands the circumstances of his father's death, also as a hotshot pilot. The movie *Dirty Dancing* is really about Baby stepping out from her overprotective father. *It's a Wonderful Life* follows George Bailey in his lifelong quest to avoid following in his father's footsteps. In the end George realizes his life really is wonderful. (And you thought it was about Christmas and an angel getting his wings.)

Disney movies are often about young people challenging Dad's authority. That's the theme in *Little*

Mermaid, Aladdin, The Lion King, Pinocchio, and *Mulan.*

You find another trope in movies like *Forrest Gump* and *The Natural*, in which a man spends his entire life searching for meaning and then, in the final minutes of the film, discovers purpose and meaning in his own new role as a father.

Then, of course, are the sons who travel back in time or plow under a cornfield or hike from the North Pole to Manhattan to connect with their dad. That describes *Back to the Future, Field of Dreams,* and *Elf.*

Finally, in one of the most fascinating plot devices, the biggest turnaround in the script focuses on a father-child relationship of a secondary character. In *Home Alone*, young Kevin endures a harrowing weekend. But the minor character experiencing the greater change is the old man next door, who reunites with his grown son in the final scene. The title character in *Ferris Bueller's Day Off* doesn't learn anything during his jam-packed day. However, Ferris's friend Cameron (whose father's Ferrari is resting in the ravine behind his house) is about to have a life-changing conversation. Cameron says, "When Morris comes home, he and I will just have a little chat. It's cool. It's going to be good." Likewise, the title character in *Mary Poppins* flies in and flies out. The movie is really about Mr. Banks learning to appreciate his children.

Try this test, Dad. Do a brief analysis of the next ten movies you see. Consider which character changes the most. Don't be surprised if eight of those films have a major plot development about fatherhood. You may not even see that father—as in *Top Gun, Ferris Bueller,* or *Rain Man*—but as with all dads, the father's presence or lack of presence is clearly felt. I'd love to hear your findings.

Home and Work

The debate over quality time versus quantity time is over. You really cannot expect to have any quality time with your children unless you have had sufficient quantity time.

The idea that we can work 70-hour weeks, ignore our kids month after month, and then make up for it with a trip to Disney World or skiing at Aspen is a myth. Your kids may have fun in Orlando or Colorado, but it won't be with you. It will be with a stranger who happens to pay the bills and gets their name right most of the time.

Is that harsh? A little. If you're like most dads, there will probably be a season of life when your job takes you away from your family for an uncomfortable number of minutes, hours, days, or weeks. Still, it doesn't have to spell disaster.

First, know that every family is different. Moms and dads all go through seasons during which balancing work and home is a challenge.

Second, your kids benefit when you model responsibility, hard work, and loyalty to an employer. And, if you're honest with them, most kids understand that sometimes Dad has to work. There's no reason to feel guilty.

Third, have a family-first attitude. When you realize work is starting to pull you away, be extra intentional about knowing what's going on in the lives of your children. Put their "can't miss" events on your calendar. Cut back on golf, softball, and other optional stuff. Make your kids your hobby. Hustle home from work and travel. Sometimes surprise them by showing up. Treat vacation time as sacred. On the job, be known as the guy who puts his family first. Maybe even pass up a promotion.

Finally, have long talks with your children's mother about what your kids need from their dad. Listen. Get on the same page. And do what's best for the entire family.

Honoring Stuff

Most stuff is just stuff. When a toy breaks, life goes on. When a pair of jeans—even a favorite pair—gets a hole in the knee, it's really okay. Toys, clothes, electronics, and sports gear have limited life spans. Dads need to encourage sharing and minimize the value put on "stuff."

But each child likely has a few possessions that need to be honored. Something they earned or worked for. Something they cherish. Something that siblings and parents shouldn't mess with.

For example, varsity baseball coaches often inject a bit of ceremony into the presentation of team caps. It's a privilege to be on the team. A privilege that comes with expectations and responsibility. At home, those ball caps shouldn't be borrowed, tossed around, or trivialized.

Also worthy of honor might be that one well-worn stuffed animal that your school-age son or daughter hugged through a minor crisis. Years later, don't pack it away with the other stuffed creatures. And certainly don't toss it or give it away.

Other items in this category might include their personal Bible, baseball glove, lacrosse stick, pendant from Grandma, lucky water bottle, or varsity letter jacket. Or maybe something they saved for and bought with their own money—a Ping putter, a Miken bat, a Cannondale mountain bike, a Pflueger rod and reel, a Gibson SJ guitar, or a Marlin 39A rimfire rifle.

Most stuff is just stuff. But your son or daughter very likely has two or three items that even Dad shouldn't borrow without asking. And you certainly don't have authority to lend those things out to a sibling who doesn't quite get the honor code.

A Hug a Day

I hug my children every day—
It helps their hearts to grow.
I love them more than words can say,
And hugs will let them know.
Every child who knows a hug
is headed in their way
Will grow into a parent
who will hug their own someday.

—Jay Payleitner

I Eat My Peas with Honey

anonymous

I eat my peas with honey;
I've done it all my life.
It makes the peas taste funny,
But keeps them on the knife.

I Have a Dream

On August 28, 1963, nearly a quarter of a million people gathered on the National Mall in Washington, DC, between the Lincoln Memorial and the Washington Monument. Here's an excerpt of the memorable speech that day by the Reverend Dr. Martin Luther King Jr.

> I have a dream that my four little children will one day live in a nation where they will not be judged by the color of their skin, but by the content of their character.

> I have a dream today!

I have a dream that one day, down in Alabama, with its vicious racists, with its governor having his lips dripping with the words of "interposition" and "nullification"—one day right there in Alabama, little black boys and black girls will be able to join hands with little white boys and white girls as sisters and brothers.

I have a dream today!

I have a dream that one day every valley shall be exalted, and every hill and mountain shall be made low, the rough places will be made plain, and the crooked places will be made straight, "and the glory of the Lord shall be revealed and all flesh shall see it together."

This is our hope, and this is the faith that I go back to the South with.

With this faith, we will be able to hew out of the mountain of despair a stone of hope. With this faith, we will be able to transform the jangling discords of our nation into a beautiful symphony of brotherhood. With this faith, we will be able to work together, to pray together, to struggle together, to go to jail together, to stand up for freedom together, knowing that we will be free one day.

And this will be the day—this will be the day when all of God's children will be able to sing with new meaning,

> My country, 'tis of thee, sweet land of
> liberty, of thee I sing.
> Land where my fathers died, land of the
> Pilgrim's pride,
> From every mountainside, let freedom
> ring!

In Flanders Fields

In Flanders fields the poppies blow
Between the crosses, row on row,
That mark our place, and in the sky,
The larks, still bravely singing, fly,
Scarce heard amid the guns below.

We are the dead. Short days ago
We lived, felt dawn, saw sunset glow,
Loved and were loved, and now we lie
In Flanders fields.

Take up our quarrel with the foe!
To you from failing hands we throw

The torch; be yours to hold it high!
If ye break faith with us who die
We shall not sleep, though poppies grow
In Flanders fields.

—John McCrae, 1872–1918

McCrae, a Canadian gunner and medical officer, wrote this poem to honor the sacrifice of Allied troops buried in Belgium during World War I. For centuries, it has been said that poppies are the first plants to grow over the graves of soldiers, especially on a battlefield where blood was shed. The poem inspired the use of poppies as the American Legion's official remembrance for fallen soldiers.

Inflating Needles

It will happen. Your son or daughter will come to you with a deflated basketball, football, volleyball, or soccer ball. Without any words, go to your desk drawer, cuff-link case, or tin can on your workbench and pull out one of those precious two-inch chrome inflating needles. You do have one, don't you? If not, pick up one (or two) in the next 48 hours and put it in a secure place that only you know about. Because when your kids are in dire straits and still in your care, you want them coming to you. Dad, never miss the chance to be an instant hero.

Invisible Force Field

You can't see it because it's invisible. But you know it's there. At the bedroom doorway of most teenagers is an invisible force field that prevents or radically hinders fathers from entering. It doesn't seem fair, I know. It's your house. You're paying the rent or mortgage. You should be able to freely walk into your teenager's room anytime you want. But you can't.

Or can you? Here are a couple methods for breaking through that nasty force field.

The best way is to start early. Do four-year-olds welcome Dad into their bedroom? Absolutely. How about six-year-olds? Nine? Eleven? If you start early and make a habit of wandering into their room a few evenings a

week, you will always be a welcome guest. Once inside, talk about life—their day or your day. Read a story. Play a game. Hold a conversation with their stuffed animals. Ask how they came up with the idea for a science project or wall hanging. Pray together. Or maybe just sit without talking, petting the dog, watching raindrops on the window, or listening to one of their favorite musical artists without judgment.

If you didn't start early and that force field is seemingly impenetrable, try this. Lean in the doorway—just outside the sting of the force field—and ask for your teenager's help.

"I'm not sure what to get Mom for Christmas. Got any ideas?"

"A friend at work has a nine-year-old daughter and wants to know what books will get her interested in reading. What would you suggest?"

"I heard there's an app that turns my iPhone into a flashlight / star finder / pedometer / TV remote / foreign language translator / guitar tuner. Can you help me?"

"Mom and I are too exhausted to cook. So it's going to be pizza, Chinese, or Chipotle. Your choice. I'll drive. Or you drive. Or we can both go."

"We're thinking about going someplace fun as a family between Christmas and New Year's. Maybe a beach. Maybe skiing. Whaddaya think?"

Asking a teenager's opinion is a powerful door opener. But if you ask, be ready to listen. Take care to not judge too quickly. Whatever the conversation that takes place in that door frame entails, end it on a positive note. Don't allow yourself to end any conversation by pushing them away. When you leave that doorway, your goal is to pull them closer to you. Make them glad you stopped by. Next time, they may even invite you in.

It Is Not the Critic Who Counts

"It is not the critic who counts; not the man who points out how the strong man stumbles, or where the doer of deeds could have done better. The credit belongs to the man who is actually in the arena, whose face is marred by dust and sweat and blood; who strives valiantly; who errs, who comes short again and again, because there is no effort without error and shortcoming; but who does actually strive to do the deeds; who knows great enthusiasms, the great devotions; who spends himself in a worthy cause; who at the best knows in the end the triumph of high achievement, and who at the worst, if he fails, at least fails while daring greatly, so that his place shall never be with those cold and timid souls who neither know victory nor defeat."

—Theodore Roosevelt[6]

> The father of a daughter is nothing but a high-class hostage. A father turns a stony face to his sons, berates them, shakes his antlers, paws the ground, snorts, runs them off into the underbrush, but when his daughter puts her arm over his shoulder and says, "Daddy, I need to ask you something," he is a pat of butter in a hot frying pan.
>
> —Garrison Keillor

Jj

Jabberwocky

'Twas brillig, and the slithy toves
    Did gyre and gimble in the wabe;
All mimsy were the borogoves,
    And the mome raths outgrabe.

"Beware the Jabberwock, my son!
    The jaws that bite, the claws that catch!

Beware the Jubjub bird, and shun
    The frumious Bandersnatch!"

He took his vorpal sword in hand;
    Long time the manxome foe he sought—
So rested he by the Tumtum tree,
    And stood awhile in thought.

And, as in uffish thought he stood,
    The Jabberwock, with eyes of flame,
Came whiffling through the tulgey wood,
    And burbled as it came!

One, two! One, two! And through and through
    The vorpal blade went snicker-snack!
He left it dead, and with its head
    He went galumphing back.

"And hast thou slain the Jabberwock?
    Come to my arms, my beamish boy!
O frabjous day! Callooh! Callay!"
    He chortled in his joy.

'Twas brillig, and the slithy toves
    Did gyre and gimble in the wabe;
All mimsy were the borogoves,
    And the mome raths outgrabe.

—Lewis Carroll[7]

Jokes to Tell Your Kids

Animal Crackers

A mom walks into the kitchen and sees her daughter has dumped a whole box of animal crackers onto the counter. She says, "What are you doing? You really should eat one at a time."

The little girl says, "But, Mom, the box says 'Do not eat if the seal is broken.' And I can't find the seal."

Busy Doctor

A man rushes into a busy doctor's office and shouts, "Doctor! I think I'm shrinking!"

The doctor calmly responds, "All right, settle down. I think we can fit you in. You'll just have to be a little patient."

Paradise Found

A little boy opens the big family Bible, carefully fingering the old pages. Suddenly, something falls out. He picks up the object and studies it carefully. It's an old oak leaf that had been pressed in between the pages.

"Mama, look what I found!" the boy calls out.

She asks, "What have you got there, dear?"

The young boy answers, "I think it's Adam's underwear!"

Before Cable

Did you hear about the two antennae who met on a roof, fell in love, and got married? The ceremony wasn't much, but the reception was excellent.

Better than GPS

A woman frantically calls the fire department to report a fire in her neighborhood. The dispatcher asks, "Okay, lady—how do we get there?"

Confused, she replies, "Don't you still have those big red trucks?"

Jordan River

Then Jesus came from Galilee to the Jordan to be baptized by John. But John tried to deter him, saying, "I need to be baptized by you, and do you come to me?"

Jesus replied, "Let it be so now; it is proper for

us to do this to fulfill all righteousness."
Then John consented.

As soon as Jesus was baptized, he went up
out of the water. At that moment heaven
was opened, and he saw the Spirit of God
descending like a dove and alighting on
him. And a voice from heaven said, "This
is my Son, whom I love; with him I am
well pleased."

—Matthew 3:13-17

Kick the Can, Hopscotch, Foursquare, and More

Red rover. Spud. Freeze tag. Red light, green light. Mother, may I. Duck, duck, goose. Hide-and-seek. Sardines. Dodgeball. HORSE. Ghost in the graveyard. Hot potato. Jacks. Marbles. Crack the whip. Tackle the man with the ball. Pickle. Sharks and minnows. Statue maker. Marco Polo. Blind man's bluff. Flashlight tag. Buck-buck. Capture the flag…

Bringing back any memories? Gather a bunch of grade school kids (and maybe a few other dads) in your backyard or on some blacktop. Teach your favorite games to the next generation. And tell them to stay outside until the streetlights come on.

Kid Yourself

Your assignment for today, Dad, is to do three of the following. Any three.

Skip. Skip rocks. Climb rocks. Climb a tree. Climb real high on a tree. Build a tree fort. Build a fort in your living room out of furniture, pillows, and blankets.

(Use an upside-down laundry basket as a lookout tower.) Blow bubbles. Blow bubblegum bubbles. Riffle through your old baseball card collection. Buy five new packs of baseball cards. Hold a tea party. Bake cupcakes. Eat a Twinkie. Dunk Oreos. Eat a baloney sandwich. Doodle. Chase the cat. Draw whiskers on your face. Meow at your wife. Play cat's cradle. Hula hoop. Play ring-around-the-rosy. Play hide-and-seek. Play hopscotch. Make paper airplanes. Make a cootie catcher. Make shadow puppets. Make snow angels. Build a snowman. Build a sand castle. Run through the sprinkler. Run through a pile of leaves. Run to your neighbor's house, ring their doorbell, and hide behind a bush. Leave them a plate of cookies. Play checkers. Play 20 questions. Read a Dr. Seuss book. Give every member of your family a burbly kiss on the cheek and ask, "Do you love me?"

Of course, and most important, don't do any of these things alone. Do them with one or more of your kids, age one to twenty-five.[8]

Kiss Your Wife in the Kitchen

Such a scandalous activity achieves three worthy goals.

1. It shows your wife that you love her.

2. It shows your children that you love their mother.

3. It demonstrates to your children that romance can exist in a committed marriage relationship.

In film and television, romance typically occurs between beautiful couples under 30. Usually very soon after they've met. On occasion, the man and woman on-screen are married. Just not to each other.

So, Dad, your assignment is to regularly kiss your wife in the kitchen. Incidentally, you know you're doing it properly if your third grader says, "Ewwww!" or your teenager says, "Get a room!"

Knotting the Napkin

Twist a cloth napkin so it looks like a rope and then lay it on the table. Challenge your child to grab both ends of the napkin and tie a knot in the center without letting go of either end.

When she tries and fails, set the napkin in front of you and surprise her with the simple solution. Cross your arms. Grab the left end of the napkin with your right hand and the right end of the napkin with your left hand. Without letting go, unfold your arms slowly and the knot will tie itself.[9]

> *Sometimes dads forget that our ultimate goal is to make ourselves obsolete— to work our way out of a job.*
>
> *—Jay Payleitner*

Living Sacrifices

Got a son or daughter who drinks alcohol, smokes pot or cigarettes, sniffs glue, huffs, dips, does hard drugs, or cuts?

I am not an expert. But I do know this. When they were little, they trusted you to feed them, keep them safe, tuck them in, and keep the monsters out of the closet. Today, they still trust you to keep them safe and keep the monsters away.

So do whatever it takes. Get help. Talk to experts. Involve other adults whom they trusted and respected in the past. Do research. If necessary, search their room, their car, and their clothes. If their life is in danger, don't worry about breaking their trust. They trust you to protect them. Consider a professionally led intervention. Read Romans 12:1-2:

> Therefore, I urge you, brothers and sisters, in view of God's mercy, to offer your bodies as a living sacrifice, holy and pleasing to God—this is your true and proper worship. Do not conform to the pattern of this world, but be transformed by the renewing of your mind. Then you will be able to test

and approve what God's will is—his good, pleasing and perfect will.

And then personalize it for your own hurting child.

Heavenly Father, in view of God's mercy, I lift up Ashley as a living sacrifice. Help Ashley's life be holy and pleasing to you, God, as a true and proper act of worship. Help Ashley not to conform to the pattern of the world, but to be transformed by the renewing of her mind. Help Ashley be able to test and approve your good, pleasing, and perfect will.

At the right time, tell your child that you are praying for them. Even ask if you can pray *with* them. Keep loving them. Don't hate them. Hate what they're doing.

Love

Love is patient, love is kind. It does not envy, it does not boast, it is not proud. It does not dishonor others, it is not self-seeking, it is not easily angered, it keeps no record of wrongs. Love does not delight in evil but rejoices with the truth.

It always protects, always trusts, always
hopes, always perseveres. Love never fails.

—1 Corinthians 13:4-8

He will turn the hearts of the parents to
their children, and the hearts of the children
to their parents; or else I will come and
strike the land with total destruction.

—Malachi 4:6

Mad Skills

A mad skill is a mildly impressive or amusing ability that probably will *not* lead directly to a large amount of cash, scholarships, job offers, or world peace.

But more often than you might imagine, a well-executed mad skill can break the ice in a tense situation, make someone smile, and even give your son or daughter just a bit more confidence and likability in their peer group.

What mad skill can you teach your son or daughter this week? Here are a few ideas.

Juggling. Whistling with your fingers. Reciting the alphabet backward. Reciting all the presidents in eight seconds. Hanging a spoon from your nose. Whirling nunchakus. Drawing caricatures. Folding a really sweet airplane out of a single sheet of paper. Identifying a few key constellations—the Big Dipper, Orion's Belt, the North Star. Performing a few simple magic tricks. Performing a few simple card tricks. Solving a Rubik's Cube. Playing the spoons. Twisting balloon animals.

Demonstrating and passing on a mad skill yields multiple rewards. You impress your kids. You spend time with them. You equip them for success in the future. You watch—typically from a distance—as they utilize that mad skill. And, perhaps best of all, sometime after the fact, they will think of you, smile, and be glad you are their dad.

Main Valve

I clearly remember my father showing me how to shut off the main water supply to the house. It was empowering. I was just a kid, but he was equipping me to take an adult responsibility. Do your kids know where your water shut-off valve is and how to use it, where your circuit breakers are and how to reset them, and where your fire extinguisher is and how to operate it? As they get older, do they know where to find critical legal documents, passwords, and a list of contacts in case of emergency?

The best part about equipping a growing child to accept new responsibility might be that it takes some of the burden off you, Dad. You may even find yourself saying things like, "Hey, Son, go down to the basement and reset the circuit breaker for the kitchen outlets, would ya?"

Memorize

Got a brilliant but bored second or third grader? At that age, they'll do anything to please their dad. And their minds are like a sponge and have not yet been filled with all the worries of the world. That's a great age to start giving them things to memorize, such as...

the planets in the solar system

John 3:16

"The Road Not Taken" by Robert Frost

the American Sign Language alphabet

the Gettysburg Address

Psalm 23

the first 20 elements on the Periodic Table

The Prayer of Saint Francis

Teddy Roosevelt's "Man in the Arena" passage (quoted on pages 78-79)

the Greek alphabet

multiplication tables through 12 times 12

Ecclesiastes 3:1-8

Bribe them if you have to. Five bucks for each one. Or try this: "Memorize such-and-such and earn an hour of screen time."

Middle Names

Pick them carefully. Make sure their initials don't spell anything weird. It's not a bad idea to honor an ancestor with your son or daughter's middle name. Take care that their first name works with or without the middle name. Our daughter, Rae Anne, is "Rae" to quite a few friends. And that's okay. My four sons share the same middle name—Jay. It just kinda happened.

Modeling

by Jeremy Gramento, Forreston, Illinois

As fathers, we often talk a big game but don't always back it up with our actions. About the time I realized I was falling short in that area, I came across a precept that helped me realign my role as a father: People may not always believe what you say, but they will believe everything you do.

From that point on—with the help of my church family at Leaf River Baptist Church—I finally began to be an influence for Christ in my home and community. My kids noticed. And so did my wife.

Movie Quotes

"Look inside yourself, Simba. You are more than what you have become. You must take your place in the Circle of Life."

—Mufasa (James Earl Jones,
The Lion King, 1994)

"Dad, I may not be the best, but I come to believe that I got it in me to be somebody in this world. And it's not because I'm so different from you either. It's because I'm the same. I mean, I can be just as hard-headed and just as tough. I only hope I can be as good a man as you."

—Homer Hickam (Jake Gyllenhaal,
October Sky, 1999)

"Oh, now, Pop, I couldn't. I couldn't face being cooped up for the rest of my life in a shabby little office...Oh, I'm sorry, Pop, I didn't mean that. But this business of nickels and dimes and spending all your life trying to figure out how to save three cents on a length of pipe...I'd go crazy. I want to do something big and something important."

—George Bailey (Jimmy Stewart, *It's a
Wonderful Life*, 1946)

"Now, I had heard that word at least ten times a day from my old man. He worked in profanity the way other artists might work in oils or clay. It was his true medium; a master."

—Ralphie (Jean Shepherd, *A Christmas Story*, 1983)

"If we don't start trusting our children…how will they ever become trustworthy? I'm told that the senior class at the high school…has gotten use of the warehouse in Bayson…for the purpose of putting on a senior dance. Please…join me to pray to the Lord to guide them in their endeavors."

—Reverend Shaw Moore (John Lithgow, *Footloose*, 1984)

"First we'll make snow angels for two hours, then we'll go ice skating, then we'll eat a whole roll of Tollhouse Cookie dough as fast as we can, and then we'll snuggle."

—Buddy (Will Farrel, *Elf*, 2003)

"Well, I guess there's one problem left—how much I'm going to miss her."

—King Triton (Kenneth Mars, *The Little Mermaid*, 1989)

"By the time I was ten, playing baseball got to be like eating vegetables or taking out the garbage. So when I was 14, I started to refuse. Could you believe that? An American boy refusing to play catch with his father?"

—Ray Kinsella (Kevin Costner, *Field of Dreams*, 1989)

"You have a little girl. An adorable little girl who looks up to you and adores you in a way you could never have imagined. I remember how her little hand used to fit inside mine. Then comes the day when she wants to get her ears pierced and wants you to drop her off a block before the movie theater. From that moment on you're in a constant panic. You worry about her meeting the wrong kind of guy, the kind of guy who only wants one thing, and you know exactly what that one thing is, because it's the same thing you wanted when you were their age. Then you stop worrying about her meeting the wrong guy, and you worry about her meeting the right guy. That's the greatest fear of all because then you lose her."

—George Banks (Steve Martin, *Father of the Bride*, 1991)

Mystery Solved

Every generation, every heart, every child, and every adult wants to know love. To find love. To rest in the arms of love.

The lifelong search is daunting, bewildering, and hazardous. Many never find it. For those forlorn individuals, the secret of love remains undiscovered. I believe the mystery is solved in 1 John, one of the last books of the Bible. When you get a chance, read all of 1 John—it's only about four or five pages long. Right now, consider this short excerpt:

> And so we know and rely on the love God has for us. God is love. Whoever lives in love lives in God, and God in them.
>
> —1 John 4:16

Did you catch that? God is love. If you know God, you know love. If you don't know Him, you can't really expect to experience the deep, satisfying kind of love for which we were created. I hope that doesn't surprise you. Instead, I hope it inspires you to dig deeper and offer love without hesitation. Love your wife, your children, your dearest friends, and, yes, even your enemies.

I don't want to get in trouble with any theologians, so I must quickly add this disclaimer. Please don't put God in a box labeled "love." Indeed, God is love. Absolutely. But add to that. God is truth. God is justice. God is life. God is mercy. God is righteousness.

All of which reminds me of the statement by the controversial theologian David Jenkins, bishop of Durham. "No statement about God is simply, literally true. God is far more than can be measured, described, defined in ordinary language, or pinned down to any particular happening."

National Anthem

Know the words. When given the chance, remove your hat, face the flag, and sing it with dignity and pride. Even if you're an "I don't sing in public" type of guy.

Noogies

One of the greatest sentences you can speak to an eight-year-old boy is this: "Have you had your noogies today?"

If he says no, then immediately rescue him from his noogie-less condition. He'll thank you for it. But maybe not for a while.

If he says yes, then you have two choices. Give him

his critical advance dose of noogies for tomorrow. Or simply say, "Thank goodness, because I'm all out. Do you have any noogies you can spare?" Then watch out.

> *Every parent is at some time the father of the unreturned prodigal, with nothing to do but keep his house open to hope.*
>
> —*John Ciardi*

Obstacles

by Corey Noder, project manager

I've got three young sons, and I have not yet passed on this wisdom from my father, but I will. If my dad saw me discouraged or heard me complaining, he would say, "No hill for a climber." Those five words made quite an impact. He was making sure I knew not to expect things to come easy. You have to learn, train, find the right path, and put in the effort. My dad wasn't

going to make the hill disappear. Instead, he taught me to be a climber.

Outside

"Hey kids, go outside and play!"

Can a twenty-first-century dad say such a thing? Why, that's almost considered child brutality these days. Outside your kids might experience bugs, snakes, sand in their sandals, grass-stained pants, muddy boots, dirt under their fingernails, windburned cheeks, a sun-burned nose, frozen snot on their scarves, a little poison-ivy rash, a mosquito bite, a skinned knee, or even a lit-tle adventure and exercise.

Even a parent's worst nightmare—the abduction of your child by a stranger—is less common than it was a generation ago. Between 1970 and 2009, every category of child victimization declined. Including

aggravated assault (down 69 percent) and child sexual abuse (down 53 percent). The chance of a child being kidnapped and murdered are about one in 1.5 million.[10] Guys, we can't paralyze our kids from enjoying the adventures of childhood by raising them in a spirit of fear.

So, yes, Dad. You can most certainly send 'em outside. Better yet, join 'em.

> *Children are a gift from the LORD;*
> *they are a reward from him.*
>
> —Psalm 127:3 NLT

Park Patrol

Go to your local park district's website. Print off a list of every park in the area. Give yourself a limited time frame—this summer, this school year, this weekend—and visit each one with your young son or daughter. Pick your favorite and declare it to be your special place.

The Phantom Tollbooth

Other than the Bible, it's the most awesomest book ever. Especially for boys. Got a boy between the ages of nine and fifteen who almost never reads? If you get him a copy of *The Phantom Tollbooth*, I guarantee he will read the entire thing more quickly than you can imagine. He'll even be sad when it's over.

Written by Norton Juster and illustrated by Jules Feiffer, the 1966 book begins with a bored young man named Milo and soon whisks him into The Lands Beyond. He joins forces with a Watchdog named Tock and meets unforgettable characters like the Whether Man, King Azaz, and the Spelling Bee. His mission is to climb the Mountains of Ignorance, conquer a slew of unconventional demons, and rescue the Princesses Rhyme and Reason.

My eldest, Alec, was named after one of the characters in the book. And I've bought and given away at least a dozen copies to boys who seemed to need a bit of encouragement. Last Christmas, my daughter bought me a limited-release collector's edition of *The Phantom Tollbooth* signed by the author and illustrator. I will cherish it forever.

If you've read it, you know what I'm talking about. If you haven't…well, wait no longer. Boys your age love it too.

Photographs

For the first 100 years of photography, every click of the camera was a precious commodity. Film and processing weren't cheap. Out of a roll of 24 frames, you might get one or two pics that were real keepers. The other 20 or so often felt like fails. But with digital cameras, the best strategy is to click early and often. Anytime you gather a few friends or family members in a festive setting, click away. Get close. Real close. Make 'em smile. As they pose, I give you permission to use my favorite line: "Hey you two! Pretend you like each other." Go ahead, try it.

Take a dozen shots of the same scene. You can delete ten of them fairly quickly, but one will stand out. The right light, the right smiles, the right twinkle in every eye…that one photo very well might be cherished for a lifetime.

Planets

Mercury
Venus
Earth
Mars
Jupiter
Saturn
Uranus
Neptune

Warning: Do not argue with your third grader when they tell you there are eight planets in our solar system. When you were growing up, Dad, there were nine. But in 2006, the International Astronomical

Union redefined "planet." And apparently Pluto no longer qualified. Along with a few other celestial bodies, Pluto is now classified as a "dwarf planet." We'll see how long that decision lasts.

As technology advances, astronomers will continue to quantify and debate the identities of heavenly bodies. Dads and kids can take comfort knowing that God "determines the number of the stars and calls them each by name" (Psalm 147:4).

Psalm 127

Unless the LORD builds a house,
    the work of the builders is wasted
Unless the LORD protects a city,
    guarding it with sentries will do no good.
It is useless for you to work so hard
    from early morning until late at night,
anxiously working for food to eat;
    for God gives rest to his loved ones.
Children are a gift from the LORD;
    they are a reward from him.
Children born to a young man
    are like arrows in a warrior's hands.
How joyful is the man whose quiver is full
    of them!
He will not be put to shame when he confronts his accusers at the city gates.

It's an amazing passage. Psalm 127 (NLT). Read it again and check out all the subtext. Because, Dad, it's about you and your family.

Let me paraphrase. It says you can work 80-hour weeks building a house and buying food, thinking you're providing for your family, but actually you're neglecting them. It says you can worry and try to protect your kids from all the nasty influences out there, but you can't do it alone. We need to trust God to protect and provide for our families. Your entire family belongs to Him anyway! Your children are a gift from God. He has specifically empowered and equipped you to sharpen them, hone them straight and true, set your feet firm, choose a target carefully for each child, hold them close to your heart, and then—hardest of all— let them fly.

In case you didn't know it, that pouch on the back of an archer that holds his arrows is called a quiver. And if you have a full quiver—lots of kids—you have a great shot at a life filled with joy. Even better, as you watch your kids grow in God's grace, they will accomplish wonderful things and make you proud. Not so you can boast, but so you can give the glory back to God.

Then even your enemies downtown by the city gates will have to admit you're not a bad guy. After all, your kids turned out pretty well.

I'm not making this up. It's all in Psalm 127.[11]

Purple Cow

I never saw a Purple Cow,
I never hope to see one,
But I can tell you, anyhow,
I'd rather see than be one!

—Gelett Burgess[12]

> *Kids are going to test you, so be ready. It's much easier to get them on the right track early, before they have learned to outsmart you.*
>
> —Jay Payleitner

Quantum Physics

I don't know anything about quantum physics. But if I did, I would definitely teach my kids something about quantum physics.

In other words, make sure your kids know a good chunk of the things you know. Especially regarding your career, passions, hobbies, and life skills. Not so they'll follow your footsteps, but because kids want and need to know a little about their old man.

We all know butcher shops, dry cleaners, construction companies, and car dealerships that have been in the same family for generations. My dentist's daughter is a dentist. Tim Sheehan and Claire Sheehan share an office just down the street.

"Should I do what Dad does?" All growing kids will consider this question for at least a day or two. In like manner, your kids should have a reasonable answer when people ask, "What does your dad do?"

Finally, when your son or daughter stands up to say a few words at your funeral, don't leave them mumbling something like, "I never really knew what my dad did…or who he was…or what he cared about."

Which brings me to this question: What will you say about your father when you are standing next to his casket? And let me add this reasonable challenge: If he's still around, is there more information you can gather for that little speech?

Questions

Your kid asks a question: "Dad, at night when there are no stars, where do they go?"

Now you may not have even considered that concept since you were four years old, but with two seconds of thought, a brilliant guy like you comes up with the answer. Articulating that answer—and thus demonstrating your brilliance—is one way to respond.

"The clouds hide them."

The question is answered. The kid is satisfied. And you can get back to whatever screen you were engaged with. But there may be a better option. How about

stirring their little mind by answering their question with a question: "Where do you think they are?"

If they hesitate, prompt them with additional questions.

"Are the stars still there?"

"How can something be there and you not see it?"

"Are your eyes open?"

"Is there something in the way?"

"What are stars anyway?"

"What if a star was a lot closer? What would it look like?"

"Could the sun be a star?"

You see where this is going, right? Then, of course, you can always insert a silly question.

"What if all the stars just decided to play hide-and-seek?"

"What if it's God's birthday and He blew out all the stars because He thought they were candles?"

As they get older, your questions can help your children dig deeper intellectually and soar higher spiritually.

"Where do the stars go during the day?"

"What's more important—the moon or the stars?"

"If you were lost, could you use the stars to help you get home?"

"How did the stars get there in the first place?"

In the give-and-take of Q&A, you will discover all kinds of teachable moments. You can even feel free to throw in a little biblical lesson once in a while.

"You know, the Bible says that if you lead others to know about God, you will shine like the stars forever" (Daniel 12:3).

"In Revelation, Jesus is called 'the bright Morning Star.' What do you think that means?" (Revelation 22:16).

Which brings us full circle to the inspiration for this brilliant method of teaching your kids to think for themselves. Quite often, Jesus answered a question with a question.

In Matthew 22, the Pharisees asked Jesus, "Is it right to pay the imperial tax to Caesar or not?" Jesus held up a denarius and replied, "Whose image is this? And whose inscription?"

In Luke 10 (NLT), an expert in the law asks, "Teacher, what should I do to inherit eternal life?" Jesus replied, "What does the law of Moses say? How do you read it?"

In Mark 8 (NLT), His disciples looked at a hungry crowd and said, "How are we supposed to find enough food to feed them out here in the wilderness?" Jesus asked, "How much bread do you have?"

So next time your kid comes to you with a question, ask yourself, what would Jesus do?

Almost always, the idea is to extend their question into a longer, engaging, mind-expanding dialogue. When they're a little bit older, you may not be around to respond to their questions with questions. But by that time, you will have taught them to silently ask themselves enough questions to thoughtfully and thoroughly consider every problem they face.

For now, they still need you, Dad, to keep asking questions.[13]

Quiz

find answers in the back of book, page 173

1. Which animal father spends 64 straight days incubating his egg until it hatches, losing as much as 44 pounds during that time?

2. On September 19, 1990, what father and son hit back-to-back home runs as the only father-son combo to play together on the same Major League team?

3. What father and son served as president of the United States of America?

4. What's the common name of the spider species *Pholcus phalangioides*?

5. What NHL great shared the professional ice with two sons?

6. What male animal has a pouch on its stomach in which to carry babies—as many as 2000 at a time during a pregnancy, which lasts from 10 to 25 days?

7. Which father and daughter have both won Oscars?

8. What father was always blue but never sad?

9. What article of clothing traces its origins to Chinese warriors in the third century BC?

10. According to Greek mythology, who was the father of the gods and the mortals?

11. Who wrote and recorded the plaintive song "Father and Son" on the 1970 album *Tea for the Tillerman*?

12. What fictional widower exhibited quiet
strength and stood up to social ostracism and
threats while teaching his children, Scout and
Jem, to respect the rights of all individuals?

> *The greatest blessing is a godly father. The
> greatest curse is the absence of one.*
>
> —Carolyn Brooks

Rr

Rainbows*

Raindrops in the air act as tiny prisms. White sunlight enters one side of each drop and is refracted (or bent) at different angles, depending on the wavelengths of light. The difference between the incoming ray and outgoing ray is unique to each color. Red is diffracted at 42 degrees, violet at 40 degrees, and so on. The circular rim created in the sky becomes a rainbow. Genesis

---

* Things dads should know just in case the kids ask.

9 records God creating rainbows as a gift to remind us of His promise that He will never again destroy all living things with a flood.

Reaching First Base*

hit
base on balls
error
fielder's choice
hit by pitch
dropped third strike
catcher's interference

Of the seven ways to reach first base, only one increases your batting average. Three lower your batting average. And three have no impact on your batting average.

The Road Not Taken

Two roads diverged in a yellow wood,
And sorry I could not travel both
And be one traveler, long I stood
And looked down one as far as I could
To where it bent in the undergrowth;

---

* Things dads should know just in case the kids ask.

Then took the
other, as just
as fair,
And having
perhaps the
better claim,
Because it was
grassy and
wanted wear;
Though as for
that the pass-
ing there
Had worn
them really about the same,

And both that morning equally lay
In leaves no step had trodden black.
Oh, I kept the first for another day!
Yet knowing how way leads on to way,
I doubted if I should ever come back.

I shall be telling this with a sigh
Somewhere ages and ages hence:
Two roads diverged in a wood, and I—
I took the one less traveled by,
And that has made all the difference.

—Robert Frost[14]

Roses Are Red

Roses are red,
Violets are blue.
Some poems rhyme,
This one doesn't.

Seven Ways to Shine
with Preschoolers

1. Be amazed when they bring you a bug,
   dandelion, or shiny rock.

2. Let them snuggle. (Some dads don't fully
   appreciate a good snuggle.)

3. The year before they enter kindergarten, give
   them a glimpse inside their future school
   building. Take them to a concert, play, open
   house, or book fair of an older sibling or
   neighbor kid.

4. As soon as your preschooler can spell a

dozen words (like "cat," "dog," "mom," "love," and the names of family members) make a crossword puzzle with all those words. Use sketches for clues.

5. Give noogies.

6. Teach them how, why, and when to dial 911.

7. Teach them a few things most kids don't learn until kindergarten or first grade so that their first teachers identify them as brilliant. Things like fractions, shapes, counting money, telling time, observing nature, the five senses, knowing opposites, finding your state and country on a map or globe, simple punctuation, and reading one-syllable words.

Seven Ways to Shine with School-Age Kids

1. Talk about stuff you did when you were their age. Successes. And failures.

2. Put a Pez dispenser in their lunch.

3. Let them sit in your lap. Or let them squeeze next to you on the couch or love seat. Even as they get older.

4. Challenge them to see who can make the best paper airplane.

5. Make stilts. This Saturday—together—
research stilt designs, head to the lumber-
yard, saw, drill, bolt, and encourage them to
walk tall. (Suddenly your eight-year-old is
looking you in the eye.)

6. Climb a tree or jungle gym with them and
just hang out. Literally.

7. Do slightly daring things with them.
Kayaking. Roller coasters. Rock climbing.
Garter snake hunting. Jumping off the high
dive. Batting cages. Bumper cars. Go-karts.
Archery. Running a 5K. Ice skating. Roller
skating. If they're not comfortable, don't
force them. Don't mock them. Praise them
for considering it and thinking it through.
Promise you'll ask again in a year. Don't forget.

Seven Ways to Shine with Teenagers

1. Make your home a hangout. Have soda pop
and pizza in the fridge, ice cream bars in the
freezer, a Ping-Pong table in the basement,
and parents (that's you) who don't hover.

2. If they are having a busy and productive
week, go ahead and do one of their big

chores for them, such as laundry, lawn mowing, or vacuuming.

3. Let them paint their room. Any color they want.

4. When ordering out, ask them what they want on the family pizza.

5. Chaperone a high-school dance. (But stay far, far away. Amazingly, eventually they will come and say hi to you!)

6. Slip your son or daughter an extra $40 as they leave for the school dance, especially if they're going to a fancy restaurant. The bill is always larger than they think it will be.

7. Write "Love You" on a sticky note and put it on their bathroom mirror.

Shackleton's Ad

As the story goes, in December 1913 celebrated explorer Sir Ernest Shackleton placed this small classified ad in the *London Times*. It has never been verified, but Shackleton's achievements are well documented.

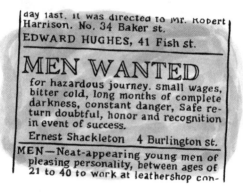

Who would answer such an advertisement? Shackleton had to turn down scores of men who responded to the offer.

One year later, Shackleton set sail with a 27-man crew with the goal of being the first to cross the continent of Antarctica. The wooden ship *Endurance* met harsher weather than expected, became locked for ten months in the ice of the Weddell Sea, and was eventually crushed by the pressure of the surrounding ice. With meager provisions, Shackleton and his entire crew camped on ice floes for five months at the mercy of the currents.

Finally drifting north into open water, the crew sailed three lifeboats to the desolate and uninhabited Elephant Island. Still 800 miles from any civilization, Shackleton and five others then sailed a 22-foot lifeboat to South Georgia Island. After that treacherous 17-day journey, they still had to hike 26 miles over mountains and glaciers to reach a whaling station on the far side of the island.

Shackleton immediately organized and led the rescue operation, returning to Elephant Island for the remainder of the crew. The most amazing part of the 21-month adventure is how it ended. Every member of Shackleton's 27-man crew made it safely home.

Dad, would you ever have answered such an ad? A better question might be, do you want your children to grow into the kind of adventurous adults who might respond to such a challenge? I think you do. Someday every son and daughter is going to face a challenge— maybe a series of challenges. They might be physical, emotional, educational, moral, or spiritual. In any case, our children need to be ready.

Especially as our kids get older, fathers need to be candid about what the future holds. So prepare them for the "hazardous journey." Warn them that Satan may besiege them with "long months of complete darkness." Promise them that if they remain faithful, they will gain "honor and recognition." In the end, when they emerge victorious, remind them to give the glory to God.

Sharing

When you go to the beach, there's no need to bring a shovel and bucket for each child. When kids are forced to share, they learn to take turns and develop patience. Do you really need more than one toaster, waffle iron, hole punch, chess set, video gaming system, Ping-Pong table, or Monopoly game in your home? I don't think so. If a fight breaks out, then no one gets to use anything. Lesson learned.

Sidestepping Fatherhood

You're an involved dad. Sure, there's always more you can do and more you can learn. But you've proactively picked up this book for dads, and that says a lot.

Unfortunately, a significant number of men have

fathered babies but are not currently plugged in as dads. Why? Well, it could be they never had a solid role model. Or they're scared. Or their child's mother has erected a barrier for some reason. Maybe these men are broke or broken. Maybe they checked out by mistake and don't know how to check back in. In my travels, I have discovered that many disconnected dads just don't realize how awesome it is to be a father.

If you know a guy who has sidestepped or retreated from his role as a father, do him a solid. Come alongside him. Show some compassion. And nudge him in such a way that he discovers the wonders and rewards of engaged fatherhood.

Invite him out for coffee or recruit him to join your men's small group. Make sure he begins to see how being a dad can be a blast. Share examples from your own life. You're not bragging or putting on a show. You're just helping him understand the joys and benefits that are readily available for any man with a son or daughter. Tell him, "Sure, it takes time. But if you put in just a little effort, the rewards come back multiplied 1000 percent!"

Can you do that, Dad? Can you be an advocate for awesome fathering? You probably know someone right now who needs a friendly nudge. That man's children will be eternally grateful.

Skiing

Dad, can you or your kids think of any other words with a double "I"? You might come up with other action words, like "taxiing" and "safariing." Or plurals, like "radii" and "genii" (a secondary spelling of "genies"). There's a mushroom called shiitake. And the game system Wii. There's even a US state with a double "I."

Or maybe you should stop thinking about such silly things and take your favorite kid snow skiing or waterskiing this very weekend. Okay, maybe take your least favorite kids too. And your bride.

Sleep

My son, do not let wisdom and understand-
ing out of your sight,
preserve sound judgment and discretion;
they will be life for you,
an ornament to grace your neck.
Then you will go on your way in safety,
and your foot will not stumble.
When you lie down, you will not be afraid;
when you lie down, your sleep will be
sweet.

—Proverbs 3:21-24

Slippery Slopes

Addicts, criminals, couch potatoes, vandals, and con artists didn't begin that way. At some point they dabbled in a counterproductive choice, and no one was there to stop them. They tried their first cigarette, shoplifted their first Snickers bar, vegged out in front of their first TV marathon, scribbled on their first wall, or lied their first lie. And they got away with it.

Those scoundrels were once at the top of a slippery slope and didn't even know it. Where was their father? Maybe he was never there. Maybe he laughed it off. Or dismissed it as just a phase. Maybe Dad even applauded the slightly deviant behavior. Some men proudly show off the office supplies or tools they stole from work or think it's their responsibility to give their son his first sip of beer.

But, Dad, you need to grab your kids early from the top of that slippery slope.

When your son first says, "Oh crap," don't wash his mouth with soap and ground him for a month. But nose-to-nose tell him to choose words more carefully.

When your daughter shoplifts a pair of sunglasses on a dare from a friend, go with her as she takes the loot back to the store. (Call ahead.)

When your four-year-old lies about shaving the cat, let him know that lying is a really big deal. You have to be able to trust him. Truth is a family imperative. Make it clear the lie itself was actually much more damaging than a cat with a reverse Mohawk.

When the swimsuit edition of your weekly sports magazine comes in the mail, take it to the garbage can and tell your son why. Say, "It's not something I need in the house. And it's not something you need either." That courageous act might even start a longer conversation with your son about how to treat women with respect.

When your daughter gets her ears pierced without your permission, sit down with her mother and talk it out. Decide together how you'll address that breach of trust.

When you discover your ten-year-old is playing video games with creepy graphics at his buddy's house, do what you have to do to make your position clear. Set some limits and stick to them.

Yes, I know it's easier to pretend you didn't see that first misstep or rationalize that it really isn't a big deal. But initial bad choices don't just go away. Most problems go from bad to worse. So beware the slippery slope.

Be the guy who rescues your precious kids before they go over the edge.

S'mores

If you have a backyard fire pit, designate a kitchen cupboard that will perpetually be stocked with marshmallows, Hershey bars, and graham crackers. Dad, you want your kids and their friends to come to your house. And maybe once in a while, they'll even invite you to join them fireside.

Sputnik*

Launched by the Russians in 1957, Sputnik was the first man-made object to circle the earth. The event's demoralizing impact on American pride is credited to have launched the space race, which the United States "won" when Neil Armstrong stepped on the moon on July 20, 1969.

The name Sputnik led to the term "beatnik," coined

---

* Things dads should know just in case the kids ask.

by Herb Caen in a 1958 newspaper article. Caen was possibly attempting to disparage the Beat Generation literary movement led by Jack Kerouac.

Squishy Ball Solicitation

Occasionally, a dad and a teenager are in the same room and the interaction is reduced to zero. The teen is distracted by some project or electronic device. The dad, sitting across the room, is yearning to make some kind of meaningful connection. He already knows that asking, "Whatcha doing?" would not end well.

The answer: the squishy ball solicitation.

Grab a Nerf or Koosh ball and simply start playing catch with yourself, probably leaning back in your couch and tossing it into the air. After much scientific research and a bit of guesswork, I've concluded that within 17 tosses there is a 93 percent chance that your teenager will look up and request a toss. It may be a nonverbal raising of an open palm. Or your teenager might even say, "Yo," or "Let's see it." When they make the squishy ball solicitation, give yourself one more toss. Examine the item as if you're deciding whether your son or daughter is toss-worthy. And then expertly flip it across the room. The more accurate the toss, the higher the chance of launching into a full-scale, father-teen interactive experience.

Hopefully Mom recognizes the value of what's going on and doesn't insist, "Yo, Children! No throwing stuff in the house." If Mom does try to thwart the interchange, you need to decide whether you will overrule her authority. That's your call.

Just to confirm, if you toss with your teen for ten minutes and no words are exchanged, that's still a great victory. Try it. And let me know how it works for you.

Statistics

- Sixty-nine percent of adults say children need a father in the home to grow up happily.[15]

- Fifty-eight percent of adults say it is "extremely important" for a father to provide values and morals to his children. Forty-one percent of adults say it is "extremely important" for a father to provide income for his children.[16]

- Since 1965, the amount of time fathers spend with their children has nearly tripled.[17]

- In 2010, 27 percent of children under age 18 were living apart from their fathers. That's up from 11 percent in 1960.[18]

- Children in father-absent homes are almost four times more likely to be poor. In 2011, 44 percent of children in mother-only families were living in poverty.[19]

- Mortality rates are 1.8 times higher for infants of unmarried mothers than for infants of married mothers.[20]

- Children who live apart from their fathers are 4.3 times more likely to smoke cigarettes as teenagers than children growing up with their fathers in the home.[21]

- Seventy-one percent of high-school dropouts are fatherless.[22]

- Seventy-five percent of all adolescent patients

in chemical abuse centers come from fatherless homes.[23]

- Seventy-two percent of adolescent murderers
  and 60 percent of America's rapists grew up
  without fathers.[24]

- Eighty-five percent of all children who
  exhibit behavioral disorders come from
  fatherless homes.[25]

Syzygy

The scientific term for the alignment of three celestial bodies is "syzygy" (pronounced SIH-zih-jee). The
most obvious examples are solar
and lunar eclipses.

In a *solar* eclipse, the
moon sneaks between
the earth and the sun,
blocking out some or
most of the sun's rays
for a short time. A solar
eclipse happens during
the day, and those who
are in the know warn
the rest of us not to look
directly at the sun. (Note to

dads: Those warnings will tempt kids to peek at the sun.)

In a *lunar* eclipse, the earth passes between the sun and the moon, casting an obvious shadow on the surface of the moon. Please don't confuse the relatively rare lunar eclipse with the phases of the moon in its monthly lunar cycle.

Just to be absolutely clear, there is no time when the sun passes between the earth and the moon. If for no other reason, it wouldn't fit. On average, the moon is about 239,000 miles away, and the diameter of the sun is approximately 865,000 miles.

Syzygy of the sun, moon, and earth may occur a few times a year. Dads who track such astronomical phenomena on the NASA website and drag their kids out of bed for a two a.m. lunar eclipse are true heroes. When your kid falls asleep in school the next day, they will probably tattle on you to the teacher. "My dad got me up for the lunar eclipse last night." But it's all good. All the other kids will be jealous.

Open doors for your children. It's their choice to walk through or not.

—Jay Payleitner

The Tortoise and the Hare

The beloved ancient Greek storyteller Aesop gave us this classic fable with a valuable moral for all ages.

There once was a hare who often bragged about how fast he could run. Tired of the boasting, a tortoise challenged him to a race. With a mocking laugh, the hare accepted. The course was set, and all the animals in the forest gathered to watch. Most of them were also tired of the hare's haughty attitude, so they rooted for the tortoise even though they knew he didn't have a chance.

The hare sprinted out to a quick lead and stopped to do a bit of gloating. He looked back at Tortoise and cried out, "How do you get anywhere at all, much less expect to win a race at such a slow-going pace?"

The hare wasn't really tired, but just to make a point about his superior speed and unbeatable lead, he stretched himself out alongside the road for a short nap. He fell asleep a little more soundly than he expected and didn't hear the quiet, steady footsteps of the tortoise plodding right past him.

As the tortoise approached the finish line, the animals were cheering so loudly, they woke up the hare. He dashed faster than he had ever run, but he was too late. The tortoise crossed the line just ahead of him—winning, as they say, by a hair.

Moral: Slow and steady wins the race.

Tree Stumps

Out walking with your kids, never pass a tree stump without jumping on it and posing like a superhero or politician and holding that statuesque stance for several seconds. The older your kids are, the louder their groans. But 25 years from now, they'll do the same thing with their own kids.

Trust

Some time later God tested Abraham. He said to him, "Abraham!"

"Here I am," he replied.

Then God said, "Take your son, your only son, whom you love—Isaac—and go to the region of Moriah. Sacrifice him there as a burnt offering on a mountain I will show you."

Early the next morning Abraham got up and loaded his donkey. He took with him two of his servants and his son Isaac. When he had cut enough wood for the burnt offering, he set out for the place God had told him about. On the third day Abraham looked up and saw the place in the distance. He said to his servants, "Stay here with the donkey while I and the boy go over there. We will worship and then we will come back to you."

Abraham took the wood for the burnt offering and placed it on his son Isaac, and he himself carried the fire and the knife. As the two of them went on together, Isaac spoke up and said to his father Abraham, "Father?"

"Yes, my son?" Abraham replied.

"The fire and wood are here," Isaac said, "but where is the lamb for the burnt offering?"

Abraham answered, "God himself will provide the lamb for the burnt offering, my son." And the two of them went on together.

When they reached the place God had told him about, Abraham built an altar there and arranged the wood on it. He bound his son Isaac and laid him on the altar, on top of the wood. Then he reached out his hand and took the knife to slay his son. But the angel of the Lord called out to him from heaven, "Abraham! Abraham!"

"Here I am," he replied.

"Do not lay a hand on the boy," he said. "Do not do anything to him. Now I know that you fear God, because you have not withheld from me your son, your only son."

Abraham looked up and there in a thicket he saw a ram caught by its horns. He went over and took the ram and sacrificed it as a burnt offering instead of his son. So Abraham called that place The Lord Will Provide. And to this day it is said, "On the mountain of the Lord it will be provided."

—Genesis 22:1-14

Tucking In

It's easy to tuck in four-year-olds. You read a story, talk about the day, say a prayer, kiss them good night, and that's it. If you dedicate the right amount of time to it—say, about 20 minutes—it can be truly magical.

With a little perseverance, a father can develop a bedtime ritual that continues until the day you drop them off at their college dorm. Over that 18-year span, the schedule will change, the topics of discussion will surely evolve, and you may miss a night or two. But if you are tenacious about tucking in your kids, you will build a connection with them that will last through the toughest times.

By the way, that time together does more than make a positive connection. It actually protects your relationship from harm. For example, you may have said some harsh words to your family during the day. Your son may have disrespected his mother after school. Your daughter may be pouting over a schoolmate's unkind words. But at bedtime, the magical moments you've had over the years will help the walls fall down, and in the glow of the night-light, you can talk it out, trade apologies, put it all in perspective, and look forward to a new day.

So start tucking in your kids, Dad. The younger, the better. But even if they're 16 or 17, go ahead, knock on their door, and ask their permission. Chances are they'll say, "Ummm…sure."

TV Dads

In 2011, *TV Guide* listed the 50 greatest TV dads of all time. What do you think of this list? How do you stack up? Ask your kids—how do they think you stack up?

Heathcliff "Cliff" Huxtable (Bill Cosby, *The Cosby Show*, 1984)

Ben Cartwright (Lorne Greene, *Bonanza*, 1959)

John Walton (Ralph Waite, *The Waltons*, 1971)

Charles Ingalls (Michael Landon, *Little House on the Prairie*, 1974)

Steven Keaton (Michael Gross, *Family Ties, 1982)*

Danny Williams (Danny Thomas, *Make Room for Daddy*, 1953)

Jim Anderson (Robert Young, *Father Knows Best*, 1954)

Steve Douglas (Fred MacMurray, *My Three Sons*, 1960)

Andy Taylor (Andy Griffith, *The Andy Griffith Show*, 1960)

Howard Cunningham (Tom Bosley, *Happy Days*, 1974)

Ray Barone (Ray Romano, *Everybody Loves Raymond*, 1996)

Eric Camden (Stephen Collins, *7th Heaven*, 1996)

Dan Conner (John Goodman, *Roseanne*, 1988)

Mike Brady (Robert Reed, *The Brady Bunch*, 1969)

Tom Corbett (Bill Bixby, *The Courtship of Eddie's Father*, 1963)

Alex Stone (Carl Betz, *The Donna Reed Show*, 1958)

Forrest Bedford (Sam Waterston, *I'll Fly Away*, 1991)

George Lopez (George Lopez, *George Lopez*, 2002)

Herman Munster (Fred Gwynne, *The Munsters*, 1964)

Tim Taylor (Tim Allen, *Home Improvement*, 1991)

Ozzie Nelson (Ozzie Nelson, *The Adventures of Ozzie and Harriet*, 1952)

Robert "Rob" Petrie (Dick Van Dyke, *The Dick Van Dyke Show*, 1961)

Tony Micelli (Tony Danza, *Who's the Boss?*, 1984)

Archie Bunker (Carroll O'Connor, *All in the Family*, 1971)

Sandy Cohen (Peter Gallagher, *The O.C.*, 2003)

Doug Lawrence (James Broderick, *Family*, 1976)

Michael Kyle (Damon Wayans, *My Wife and Kids*, 2001)

Ward Cleaver (Hugh Beaumont, *Leave It to Beaver*, 1957)

Jack Bristow (Victor Garber, *Alias*, 2001)

Chester A. Riley (Jackie Gleason, *The Life of Riley*, 1949)

Andy Sipowicz (Dennis Franz, *NYPD Blue*, 1993)

Lucas McCain (Chuck Connors, *The Rifleman*, 1958)

Tom Bradford (Dick Van Patten, *Eight Is Enough*, 1977)

Philip Banks (James Avery, *The Fresh Prince of Bel-Air*, 1990)

Homer Simpson (Dan Castellaneta, *The Simpsons*, 1989)

Rick Sammler (Billy Campbell, *Once and Again*, 1999)

Jason Seaver (Alan Thicke, *Growing Pains*, 1985)

John Robinson (Guy Williams, *Lost in Space*, 1965)

Martin Lane (William Schallert, *The Patty Duke Show*, 1963)

Will Girardi (Joe Mantegna, *Joan of Arcadia*, 2003)

Jim Walsh (James Eckhouse, *Beverly Hills, 90210*, 1990)

Fred G. Sanford (Redd Foxx, *Sanford and Son*, 1972)

Andy Brown (Treat Williams, *Everwood*, 2002)

George Jefferson (Sherman Hemsley, *The Jeffersons*, 1975)

Joseph "Rocky" Rockford (Robert Donley, *The Rockford Files*, 1974)

Michael Steadman (Ken Olin, *thirtysomething*, 1987)

Bernie "Mac" McCullough (Bernie Mac, *The Bernie Mac Show*, 2001)

Paul Hennessy (John Ritter, *8 Simple Rules*, 2002)

Graham Chase (Tom Irwin, *My So-Called Life*, 1994)

Benjamin Sisko (Avery Brooks, *Star Trek: Deep Space Nine*, 1993)

Disclaimers: Many of these fictional dads actually seem to have their act together. Quite a few I've never seen and probably never will. Some I came to appreciate in reruns. Some I am embarrassed to admit I have seen, and I cannot endorse them in any way, shape, or form. Since this list was published a few years ago, perhaps some current TV dads are worthy.

Any discussion about TV fathers with your children should probably include two key reminders. The actors' thoughtful, caring words were scripted, and most of life's problems cannot be solved in 30 or 60 minutes.

My biggest question: How can any list of TV dads be complete without Danny Tanner (Bob Saget, *Full House*) and Eric Taylor (Kyle Chandler, *Friday Night Lights*)?

Twinkling*

Stars appear to twinkle because their light passes through several miles of Earth's atmosphere before it reaches your eye. Turbulence creates churning streams and eddies in our atmosphere that act like lenses and prisms, shifting the incoming starlight from side to side by tiny amounts several times per second. For the moon, a much larger object in the night sky, these deviations average out and don't appear to cause any perceptible twinkle.

---

* Things dads should know just in case the kids ask.

> *If you want to build a ship, don't drum up the men to gather wood, divide the work, and give orders. Instead, teach them to yearn for the vast and endless sea.*
>
> —*Antoine de Saint-Exupéry*

Ultimate Compliment

"Wow. I wish I'd thought of that."

Unconditional Love

Are you loving your kids with no strings attached?

They need to know that nothing they do could make you love them any less. And nothing they do could make you love them any more.

It doesn't matter how much love you received from your parents. God has given you an endless supply, and the more you give, the more you get. When kids bring home straight A's, love them. When kids spill their milk, love them. When teenagers wreck the car, score a touchdown, ignore curfew, get elected prom queen, mow the grass without being asked, or come home pregnant, love them.

Maintain high expectations, enforce family rules, provide consequences, hold them accountable, and dare to discipline. But love them through it. Brag to your friends, post their report cards on the fridge, keep a scrapbook of their athletic achievements, and praise them for their successes. But make sure they know you love them for who they are and not what they do.

By the way, unconditional love is the perfect description of God's love for each of us.

Unicycle

Buy a unicycle for your ten-year-old. If they master it, awesome. If they give it a good effort but really can't stay balanced more than three or four seconds, that's okay. If they look at it, shake their head, and never really put any significant effort into it, that's also okay. Never make them feel bad for not achieving something that would probably take quite a bit of effort and may not even be possible for some kids. You can't look at a child and tell if they have the mental gyroscope required to balance and pedal a unicycle.

As a matter of fact, the chance that your child will master the one-wheeled beast is pretty slim. So why would I make such a suggestion? Our job as dads is to open doors for our kids. Some they will choose to walk through, some they won't. And for a certain length of time, you want them to occasionally try new things, practice, fail, try again, and push themselves to their limits right there on your driveway. Or in your backyard. Or in your basement.

That's how they find out what they're good at, which is important information when it comes to shaping their future.

That's also where they learn that it's okay to try things and fail. Which is even more important in shaping their entire life.

Unplug the TV

If you sense your son is becoming addicted to *SportsCenter* or your daughter can't live without the latest reality show or teen romance fluff, call a TV time out. Yes, it's a daring move.

Try unplugging the set for the first week of school, the entire month of June, or even just a long weekend. If they're still in elementary school, simply assert your parental authority and be ready to step in with some fun non-TV options for the entire family. If they're teenagers, be ready for some significant pushback. Explain that it's not a punishment. It's a kind of fast—good for the heart, mind, and soul. Tell them it's a good way to clear their head and begin to think their own thoughts again. Don't tell them it's a good way to reconnect with sibling and parents. That will only increase the volume of any groans or whining.

You might find it helpful to launch any period of television abstinence by taking the entire crew to a beach, campground, or resort where TVs are nowhere to be found. If it works, make it an annual event.

Then see if you can arrange a period of family abstinence from smartphones, iPads, and laptops. Good luck with that.

Vacation Driveway Checklist

As a public service to men and their families, following is my unofficial, not-yet-patented vacation checklist.

Phones, chargers, wallets, purses, glasses, prescriptions, sunglasses, laptops, computer cords, keys, watches, maps, directions, GPS, credit cards, coupons, shoes, socks, belts, hanging clothes, shaving kits, sunscreen, swimsuits, towels, hats, gifts, pillows, blankets, deodorant, girls' stuff, shaving kits, clean underwear, reading material, munchies for the car.

Say it fast even as you leave the driveway. The list varies depending on destination—beach vacations, out-of-town weddings, or camping trips. The list also comes in handy when you leave hotels and beach houses heading for home. Once you start mentioning items you can pick up cheap at any drugstore, you can stop talking.

Try it on your next trip. Sooner or later, you'll be a hero for rescuing an entire journey. The one potential problem is that your family starts to expect it. Heading down the driveway, you rattle off your vacation checklist and happen to forget one item, and that one item, of course, is the one that is forgotten. Somehow, you'll be the one taking the blame.[26]

Versatility

There's something noble about pursuing a single dream with laser-like focus. That's often what it takes to become a world-class anything.

On the other hand, it's unhealthy for any child to get stuffed in a box at an early age and slapped with a label, such as math nerd, superjock, bookworm, class clown, politician, band geek, techie, skater, rocker, cheerio, or drama geek.

Whether their box is comfy or not so much, all kids need to know they very likely have many other facets. They have other talents and gifts to explore. Leonardo da Vinci was a well-respected artist but didn't rest on those accolades. He was also a mathematician, mapmaker, civil engineer, botanist…and the inventor of musical instruments, hydraulic pumps, a steam cannon, and several flying machines. More recently, A.C. Gilbert invented the Erector set only after working his way through Yale Medical School as a magician and winning an Olympic gold medal in the pole vault. Dr. William Moulton Marston was a Harvard-educated psychologist but also invented the modern lie detector and created *Wonder Woman*.

In your own neighborhood, you might very well find an English teacher who makes cabinets, a marketing manager who collects butterflies, or a football coach who plays bass guitar in a cover band.

And, Dad, I'm thinking you might also have some latent gifts and talents ready to be unleashed that would inspire your kids. Which might substantially invigorate your own next season of life.

Virtues

You can blah, blah, blah all day and night to your kids about moral choices, but sharing well-written fiction or examples from real life may be your most effective teaching tool.

May I recommend the 830-page hardcover by William J. Bennett, *The Book of Virtues*. This bestselling anthology contains hundreds of stories and readings from great works of literature and decisive turning points in history. Entries are categorized by ten character traits, such as compassion, loyalty, perseverance, courage, and faith. Bennett pulls writings from mythology, fairy tales, fables, speeches, philosophy, poetry, short stories, and the Bible.

You can flip open to any page and find a truth or tale to share with your kids anytime. Especially at

bedtime. Keep the book readily available, and its entic-
ing pages just might lure your son or daughter away
from their favorite screen for an hour or two. Time and
time again.

Other cherished anthologies that have inspired
young people over the years include *A Treasury of Children's Literature* by Arman Eisen, *Foxe's Book of Martyrs*
by John Foxe, and *Jesus Freaks* by D.C. Talk and The
Voice of the Martyrs.

> *I believe that what we become depends on
> what our fathers teach us at odd moments,
> when they aren't trying to teach us.*
>
> —*Umberto Eco*

Waffles

See if you can find where waffles are described in
Deuteronomy 6:6-7.

> These commandments that I give you today are to be on your hearts. Impress them on your children. Talk about them when you sit at home and when you walk along the road, when you lie down and when you get up.

I'm pretty sure the last few words of that passage are a direct command for you to make waffles for your kids tomorrow morning and make it a point to talk about God's commandments. Try it.

Waiter, Waiter, There's a Fly in My Soup.

"Quiet, sir. All the other diners will want one."

"Don't worry. He won't eat much."

"Don't worry. We won't charge you extra for it."

"What do you expect for 85 cents, a beetle?"

"Sir, didn't you see the No Pets Allowed sign?"

"No, I believe that's a vitamin bee. This is a health-food restaurant."

"Hmm? That's strange—he was supposed to be in your salad."

"Oh dear, the frog must have missed it."

"Oh dear, he must have committed insecticide."

"Oh, no. Who will look after his family?"

"Don't worry, sir. The spider on your bread stick will soon take care of it."

"Yes, he's practicing the backstroke for the insect Olympics."

"No, sir, that's a cockroach. The fly is on your steak."

"That's not possible, sir. The cook used them all in the raisin bread."

"My apologies. I must have missed him when I picked out the other three."

"Of course, sir. It's fly soup."

"Of course, sir. That's how we lured the turtle into the soup pot."

"So sorry. You ordered cream of mosquito, didn't you?"

"Don't worry, sir. The goldfish will eat him before you know it."

"Well, quick—throw him a Cheerio so he won't drown."

The clever dad (that's you) will quickly come up with several ways to use this list of snappy comebacks. Try a different joke the next 20 times you have soup at home. Organize a comedy workshop by assigning punch lines to your favorite silly third grader and 19 friends. Or do an analytical review of humor with your family. Read them all out loud, discuss, and vote which response is funniest and why.

Caution: Please do not use these snappy retorts in a fancy restaurant, especially in an attempt to get soup for free.

Work

by James Read, creative director

My dad often reminded me, "You need to learn to work." I didn't like to hear it as a child, but that directive helped me learn to follow through and finish a task. I've tried to pass that on to my boys as well. The will to work doesn't come naturally—it's something we each must learn to do. Looking back, I value my father's commitment in that area.

Workmanship

*by Ron Preston, vice president,
Corrosion Monitoring Services*

When I entered the workforce, my dad gave me three pieces of advice that have served me well. I will pass this advice on to my children.

1. Work is a privilege, not a right.

2. In an eight-hour day, give nine hours of work.

3. Care about your work. It shows even if you don't notice.

Wrigley Field Wisdom

It was the annual Payleitner pilgrimage to the shrine at Clark and Addison. Growing up, my dad made sure we made it to at least one Chicago Cubs doubleheader every summer. I was nine years old.

One of the great traditions for my brother and me was filling out our own scorecards with two fresh, sharp Cubs pencils purchased from one of the vendors just inside the Wrigley Field turnstiles. In the 1960s, the scorecards were a quarter, and the pencils were a dime. We never asked our dad for foam fingers, Cubs

DAD HALL of FAME

CHICAGO CUBS

THE EMERGENCY SHARPENING OF
THIS PENCIL AT WRIGLEY FIELD DEMONSTRATED
A DAD'S GENIUS TO HIS SON.

pennants, or Billy Williams jerseys. We knew those scorecards and pencils were our souvenirs. And that was enough.

On this particular outing, about the second inning, tragedy struck. My pencil lead broke. Of course, I could sharpen it at home, but how was I going to complete my traditional duties tracking Kessinger, Beckert, Williams, Banks, Santo, Hundley, and company? I couldn't ask for another pencil, could I?

I showed the unusable writing utensil to my dad, and he didn't miss a beat. He took it and within 20 seconds handed it back sharpened and ready for the next batter. You may be able guess what he did. To an adult, it may seem obvious. But to this nine-year-old, scraping that pencil at just the right angle with just the right pressure against the concrete floor of the grandstand was nothing short of brilliant. My dad was a genius!

Dad, take advantage of those years when you know more about life than your kids. Solve the occasional minor crisis. Display creativity and wisdom. Earn their confidence. Be a humble hero. Store up your genius points so you can cash them in later when the challenges of life get a little more complicated and have greater consequences for your kids.[27]

> *Train up a child in the way he should go;*
> *even when he is old he will not depart from it.*
>
> —*Proverbs 22:6* ESV

XXXXXXXXXX
(Ten Kisses)

These ten classic goodnight kisses are the perfect way to end the day with daughters *and* sons. Of any and all ages. With any luck, they'll kiss you back in their own creative way.

1. *Fish kiss.* Playfully peck at your child with thin, puckered lips.

2. *Butterfly kiss.* Tickle their cheek tenderly with blinking eyelashes. Invite them to give their own fluttery eyelash kisses.

3. *Eskimo kiss.* Gently rub noses.

4. *Blow a kiss.* Stand at a distance, place a kiss on your fingertips, and blow it in their direction.

5. *Throw a kiss.* Stand at a distance, place a kiss on your fingertips, wind up, and hurl away.

6. *Kiss monster.* Make strange snarls, growls, and silly faces as you place fast and funny kisses all over their face.

7. *Raspberry surprise.* Lean in to kiss their cheek, but plant a giant, burbling raspberry instead.

8. *Miss kiss.* Announce that you are kissing their cheek, but kiss their ear. Announce you are kissing their forehead, but kiss their hair. Announce you are kissing their lips, but kiss their nose.

9. *Motor kiss.* Tug your ear several times like a sputtering motor. Then finally start your lips flapping noisily until they make contact with their cheek.

10. *Bait and switch.* Ask them for a kiss on the cheek. Turn your head at the last moment so their kiss lands on your lips.[28]

Yearbooks

Has it been a while since you shared a good laugh with your high-schooler? Pull out your old yearbook and leave it on the kitchen table. And get ready for some zingers.

As they scan the ancient photographs, read the printed text, and decipher notes and autographs scribbled by classmates, they will have numerous questions. Your goal is to answer your teenager's questions as honestly as possible.

"How did you get that nickname?"

"Were you a geek, or did you just look like one?"

"What did you do to get kicked out of Mrs. Bannon's homeroom?"

"Who's TJ?"

"Why won't TJ ever forget what happened after the homecoming game?"

"Did you go to the prom and the homecoming dance? Which girl did you take?"

"So, this girl, Carol, who clearly had a crush on you…was she a good kisser?"

"Does Mom know about Carol?"

"When's the last time you talked to Carol, Wendy, or Gina? Let's Google them!"

Go ahead and encourage their questions. The best part of conversations like these is that any question they ask you, you can ask a similar one of them.

Yeti Tracks

Cut giant footprints out of plywood, complete with pointy claws. After a fresh snowfall, attach them

to your boots and take long strides across your lawn. In the morning, let your son or daughter discover the abominable evidence and be scared out of their wits! After a suitable amount of detective work and speculation (maybe an hour, maybe a year), reveal your handmade sasquatch-footprint maker. Beg their forgiveness—and then help them make a frightening monster trail across the lawns of the entire neighborhood!

Don't have snow in your area? Try making giant monster footprints on a beach before the crowds come or muddy tracks across your neighbor's driveway.

Your Dad

After speaking with men all over the country, it's pretty clear that every dad is unique.

I've heard lots of good stuff. Men who put their families first. Dads who are a blast to hang out with.

Dads who work long hours but still somehow find the time to make memories. Dads who discipline with love and compassion. Dads who challenge their sons and daughters to reach for the stars. Men who aren't afraid to stand up for truth and aren't afraid to cry when their hearts are broken. Men who really step it up in a crisis. Fathers who sit on the edge of every bed in the house just about every night, pray heartfelt prayers, and whisper, "I love you so much."

I've heard some bad stuff too. And as we approach the end of this book filled with encouragement for hardworking dads, I'm just not going there. It's too much of a drag.

And then there's your dad.

He wasn't perfect. No father is. He did the best he could. And really, there's no way you can ever know every life experience that shaped him into the kind of dad he was.

For better or worse, his life made an indelible impression on your mind and heart. He left you with a heritage, complete with all kinds of attitudes, opinions, virtues, and vices. Some good. Some not so good. You need to ask yourself and decide, What am I going to hang on to? What am I going to cast aside?

Hint: Keep things like integrity, generosity, gratitude, gentleness, respect, diligence, and love. Rid yourself of things like laziness, rage, envy, racism, spite, faultfinding, and vulgarity.

So take a long look at your family history. Choose to pass on the best of it as your legacy. Allow the less than ideal stuff to fade into history. Learn from it and move on.

Here's the point. Dad, your heritage has been defined by others. It has limits and liabilities. But your legacy has not yet been written.

> *Discipline your children,*
> *and they will give you peace;*
> *they will bring you the delights you desire.*
>
> —*Proverbs 29:17*

Zz

Zoo Splurge

Going to the zoo isn't cheap. Which means once Dad pays for parking and admission, he spends the rest of the day saying no to additional expenses. No to souvenirs. No to snacks. No to the dolphin show, petting area, or monkey mania. And that's okay. Really, kids need to learn they can't have everything they ask for. As a matter of fact, they need to learn to stop asking! (And whining is never permitted.)

But on at least one of those trips, before you enter the gates, announce, "Zoo Splurge!" Budget an extra wad of cash and let your whole family know you will very likely say yes to just about anything and everything.

Does that idea frighten you? Dad, you may discover your kids don't go as crazy as you think. There's a good chance their choices and purchases will be thoughtful and reasonable. If it goes well, follow that up with a Ballpark Splurge, County Fair Splurge, Bookstore Splurge, Theme Park Splurge…

The best part of the occasional splurge is that you will have an easier time enforcing limits and reducing requests and whining on future visits to the park, fair, store, and zoo. You can even announce, "Hey, gang, this is not a splurge event."

Finally, if you're the kind of dad who already overindulges your kids on most family outings, try a Reverse Splurge. That would be going to the zoo and doing *only* what comes with regular admission. No sno-cones. No stuffed koalas. No extra shows. Your kids may discover they can have fun without all the extras.

Zoom

You've heard it before, but it cannot be emphasized enough. Your kids are with you for an incredibly short season. Yes, sometimes the clock ticks slowly. One particular day may seem painfully long. A sleepless night with a sick child can feel interminable. But the calendar turns quickly. Truly the years fly by. *Zoom.*

Take lots of photos. Keep a file folder of scribbles, drawings, and programs. Hang on to that ticket stub.

Treasure that sticky note from your son. Cherish that handmade Valentine from your daughter. Keep every promise. Be there at every chance. Don't let a misunderstanding or minor disagreement with your son or daughter keep you apart for more than a moment. Your time together is too precious for such nonsense.

Dad, collar that sprinting timepiece. You have the power to slow it down. Choose to cherish this day. Appreciate the small moments. The baby giggles. Your daughter twirls through the kitchen. Your son puts his hand on your shoulder and asks a question. Did you treasure the beauty in each moment?

Maybe even step outside yourself and view your family as an outsider might. You're doing a great job, Dad. Keep at it.

And hey, if God gives you an idea on how to connect with your child this weekend, don't let anything get in the way. This weekend only happens once. *Zoom.*

Fathering Quiz Answers

answers to quiz on pages 116–18

1. the emperor penguin

2. Ken Griffey and Ken Griffey Jr.

3. John Adams and John Quincy Adams, the second and sixth presidents, and George H.W. Bush and George W. Bush, the forty-first and forty-third presidents

4. daddy longlegs

5. Gordy Howe and his sons Mark and Marty

6. the seahorse

7. John Houston and Angelica Houston, Vincent Minelli and Liza Minelli, Francis Ford Coppola and Sophia Coppola, and Henry Fonda and Jane Fonda

8. Papa Smurf

9. the necktie

10. Zeus

11. Cat Stevens

12. Atticus Finch in *To Kill a Mockingbird*

1. Adapted from Giovanni Livera and Ken Preuss, *The Amazing Dad* (New York: Perigee Trade, 2001), 147.

2. From Edgar Albert Guest, *The Passing Throng* (Chicago: Reilly & Lee, 1923), np.

3. "Paco...All Is Forgiven," *The Christian Post*, February 4, 2007, www.christianpost.com/news/paco-all-is-forgiven-25617/.

4. Cited in "Thanks, Dad: Anecdotes on the Men Who Raised Us," gearpatrol.com/2013/06/06/dear-dad-gps-fathers-day-anecdotes.

5. Excerpted in part from Jay Payleitner, *One-Minute Devotions for Dads* (Eugene: Harvest House, 2012), 115-16.

6. From Roosevelt's "Citizenship in a Republic" speech, delivered at the Sorbonne in Paris, France, on April 23, 1910.

7. From Lewis Carroll, *Through the Looking-Glass, and What Alice Found There* (New York: Macmillan, 1871).

8. Excerpted in part from Payleitner, *One-Minute Devotions for Dads*, 99-100.

9. Adapted from Livera and Preuss, *The Amazing Dad*, 143.

10. David Villand, "The Kids Really Are All Right," *Pacific Standard*, May 28, 2013, www.psmag.com/culture/the-kids-really-are-all-right-58651/.

11. Adapted from Jay Payleitner, *52 Things Kids Need from a Dad* (Eugene: Harvest House, 2010), 131-32.

12. Cited in Carolyn Wells, ed., *Book of Humorous Verse* (New York: George H. Doran, 1936), 732.

13. Adapted from Payleitner, *52 Things Kids Need from a Dad*, 45-47.

14. "The Road Not Taken" is the first poem in Robert Frost's collection *Mountain Interval* (New York: Henry Holt, 1916).

15. Paul Taylor et al., "A Tale of Two Fathers," Pew Research Center, June 15, 2011, www.pewsocialtrends.org/files/2011/06/fathers-FINAL-report.pdf.

16. "The New American Father," Pew Research Center, June 14, 2013, www.pewsocialtrends.org/2013/06/14/the-new-american-father/.

17. Kim Parker and Wendy Wang, "Modern Parenthood," Pew Research Center, March 14, 2013, www.pewsocialtrends.org/2013/03/14/modern-parenthood-roles-of-moms-and-dads-converge-as-they-balance-work-and-family/.

18. Taylor et al., "A Tale of Two Fathers."

19. Cited in "Father Facts," National Fatherhood Initiative, www.fatherhood.org/father-absence-statistics.

20. "Father Facts."

21. Warren R. Stanton et al., "Sociodemographic Characteristics of Adolescent Smokers," *The International Journal of Addiction* 7, 1994, 913-25. Cited in "Fatherhood," Palmetto Family, www.palmettofamily.org/Father6.asp.

22. Edward Kruk, "Father Absence, Father Deficit, Father Hunger," *Psychology Today*, May 23, 2012, www.psychologytoday.com/blog/co-parenting-after-divorce/201205/father-absence-father-deficit-father-hunger.

23. Cited in "Statistics of a Fatherless America," *Dads4kids.com*, www.photius.com/feminocracy/facts_on_fatherless_kids.html.

24. Cited in "Statistics of a Fatherless America."

25. Cited in "Statistics of a Fatherless America."

26. Adapted from Payleitner, *52 Things Kids Need from a Dad*, 105-6.

27. Adapted from Payleitner, *One-Minute Devotions for Dads*, 19-20.

28. Adapted from Livera and Preuss, *The Amazing Dad*, 190-91.

The National Center for Fathering

We believe every child needs a dad they can count on. At the National Center for Fathering, we inspire and equip men to be the involved fathers, stepfathers, grandfathers, and father figures their children need.

The National Center was founded by Dr. Ken Canfield in 1990 as a nonprofit scientific and education organization. Today, under the leadership of CEO Carey Casey, we continue to provide practical, research-based training and resources that reach more than one million dads annually.

We focus our work in four areas, all of which are described in detail at fathers.com:

Research. The Personal Fathering Profile, developed by a team of researchers led by Ken Canfield, and other ongoing research projects provide fresh insights for fathers and serve as benchmarks for evaluating the effectiveness of our programs and resources.

Training. Through Championship Fathering Experiences, Father-Daughter Summits, online training, small-group curricula, and train-the-trainer programs, we have equipped more than 80,000 fathers and more than 1000 trainers to impact their own families and local communities.

Programs. The National Center for Fathering provides leading-edge, turn-key fathering programs, including WATCH D.O.G.S. (Dads Of Great Students), which involves dads in their children's education and is currently in more than 1300 schools in 36 states. Other programs include Fathering Court, which helps dads with significant child-support arrearages, and our annual Father of the Year essay contest.

Resources. Our website provides a wealth of resources for dads in nearly every fathering situation, many of them available free of charge. Dads who make a commitment to Championship Fathering receive a free weekly e-newsletter full of timely and practical tips on fathering. Today's Father, Carey Casey's daily radio program, airs on more than 600 stations. Listen to programs online or download podcasts at fathers.com/radio.

Make your commitment to Championship Fathering

Championship Fathering is an effort to change the culture for today's children and the children of coming generations. We're seeking to reach, teach, and unleash 6.5 million dads, creating a national movement of men who will commit to love their children, coach their children, model for their children, encourage other children, and enlist other dads to join the team. To make the Championship Fathering commitment, visit fathers.com/cf.